# ABRAHAM'S BIND

# THE HOLY LAND
## Abram to Joseph

Hobah

Gozan
Haran
(Aram Nahariim
Paddan-aram)

Mount Lebanon

Mount Hermon

Damascus

Dan

Assyria
Mesopotamia

THE

GREAT

SEA

Dor

River
Euphrates

Oak of
Moreh

Sea of
Chinnereth

Dothan

Plain of Sharon

CANAAN

SHECHEM

River Jordan

Succoth Penuel Mahanaim

River Jabbok

Mount Gilead

Joppa

beth'El

Ai

Valley of
Shaveh

Mountain
of Mariah

Oak of
Mamre

Machpelah

Hebron
(Kiriath-
arba)

SEA of ARABAH
(Salt Sea)

Ur

Gaza

Gerar

EGYPT
River Nile

Stream of Egypt

Beersheba

Sodom (?)

Lake Menzaleh
Bitter Lakes

Goshen
Heliopolis

O Rehoboth (?)

Har
Dimona

Gomorrah (?)

Wilderness of Shur
Way to Shur

NEGEB

Zoar

Lahai Roi (?)

Seir

Wilderness
of Paran

# ABRAHAM'S BIND

## & Other Bible Tales of Trickery, Folly, Mercy and LOVE

### MICHAEL J. CADUTO

*Walking Together, Finding the Way*®
SKYLIGHT PATHS®
PUBLISHING
Woodstock, Vermont

*Abraham's Bind:*
*& Other Bible Tales of Trickery, Folly, Mercy and Love*

2006 First Printing

**Library of Congress Cataloging-in-Publication Data**
Caduto, Michael J.
Abraham's bind & other Bible tales of trickery, folly, mercy, and love / Michael J. Caduto.
p. cm.
ISBN-13: 978-1-59473-186-0 (hardcover)
ISBN-10: 1-59473-186-1 (hardcover)
1. Bible stories, English—O.T. Genesis. I. Title. II. Title: Abraham's bind and other Bible tales of trickery, folly, mercy, and love.

BS551.3.C33 2006
222'.1109505—dc22

2006017959

10   9   8   7   6   5   4   3   2   1

The story about Raven and Fox (Abu l'Hssein) that appears on pp. 22–24 is used with permission from *Earth Tales from Around the World*, © 1997 by Michael J. Caduto. Fulcrum Publishing, Golden, Colorado. All rights reserved.

Map of the Holy Land on p. ii © 2006 Michael J. Caduto.

Manufactured in the United States
Jacket Design: Sara Dismukes

SkyLight Paths Publishing is creating a place where people of different spiritual traditions come together for challenge and inspiration, a place where we can help each other understand the mystery that lies at the heart of our existence.

SkyLight Paths sees both believers and seekers as a community that increasingly transcends traditional boundaries of religion and denomination—people wanting to learn from each other, *walking together, finding the way.*

SkyLight Paths, "Walking Together, Finding the Way," and colophon are trademarks of LongHill Partners, Inc., registered in the U.S. Patent and Trademark Office.

*Walking Together, Finding the Way®*
Published by SkyLight Paths Publishing
A Division of LongHill Partners, Inc.
Sunset Farm Offices, Route 4, P.O. Box 237
Woodstock, VT 05091
Tel: (802) 457-4000      Fax: (802) 457-4004
www.skylightpaths.com

This book is dedicated
to every soul
who has ever seen the face of God
in the beauty of nature,
or in the face of a child,
and whose hand is guided
by the heart of compassion.

# Contents

# Introduction

F aith is timeless. It is particular to no person or place, no culture or
world. Faith is the hope and striving of humankind to connect
with the spirit, the oneness of all, the Creator. It is a shooting star that
streaks across the sky of our hearts and lingers there, never to depart.

From the intimate story of Abram and Sarai to the epic tale of
Joseph, this is the arc of that striving. It begins with the passionate
struggles of these individuals from an earlier time and reaches across
the generations. At its heart, these stories are a living prayer—a hunger
for love and a longing to believe in, and remain faithful to, the covenant
with Yahweh.

Who has not embarked on a new journey with trepidation and
uncertainty, as Abram does when he leads his people into the land of
Canaan? Like Isaac and Rebekah, what young lovers have not waded
into the deep emotional sea of marriage, whose tides ebb and flow
from the luminous years of courtship and promise to a deeply satisfy-
ing yet often wistful maturity? How many couples have felt the
anguish of trying to conceive and start a family while watching the
years creep past? Who has not puzzled over the paradox of deep
familial loyalties and bonds that are sometimes riven by sibling
rivalry? How often have we overcome these powerful, destructive
forces by freeing the love and mercy we feel in our hearts?

Families have often discovered the healing power and bonds of
joy that are forged by a sense of humor. Sarah laughs when Yahweh
says that she will bear a son in her old age, then she denies that she

laughed and names her son Isaac, "God has smiled." Jacob tricks his father into giving him the blessing and inheritance that was intended for his brother, Esau. Then, after working and waiting for seven years to wed Rachel, his true love, Jacob is deceived by his uncle Laban into marrying Rachel's sister, Leah.

Little has changed over the millennia. Our existence remains suspended between the realm of the eternal and the elemental plane of the material world. This tension pulls at our hearts and minds as we attempt to find our true selves in relationship to each other and to God. This is the crucible of our lives: the true test of our powers of strength and conviction in the face of adversity, our wrestling with the range of human emotion, from jealousy and rage to kindness, sacrifice, and generosity toward the ones we love.

Like our biblical forebears, we wander in the wilderness of our own search for faith. The twists and turns of this present sojourn across distant biblical lands mark a spiritual path that informs and enlightens our own journeys, leading us to a destination as mysterious and ineffable as a starry vision in the desert night. Will we find the faith and strength of spirit to follow that vision, to embark on an adventure into the ecstasy of the unknown?

# ABRAM AND SARAI

*I will bless her and give you a son by her.*
*I will bless her and she shall be the mother of nations.*

Genesis 17:16

# Prologue

Abram sat in his tent upon a camel-skin blanket, holding a bloody knife in his left hand. The ebbing sun set the tent aglow with a ruddy hue. For most of the day, coming one at a time, his kinsmen had entered the tent to join in the covenant with Yahweh. The tent smelled of smoke and blood.

Abram wiped the blade with a clean portion of the cloth that lay before him then moved it back and forth through the flames until he was satisfied that the cutting edge was purified. He studied the two finely wrought oak leaves that formed the golden hilt.

"It is time," Abram said sharply. "Enter." A man drew back the cloak that hung over the door, and Abram was momentarily blinded by the intense rays of the sun. The man reflexively raised the back of his hand to his nose as the strong, strange smell greeted him—a smell that reminded him of the altar on which slaughtered animals were burnt as offerings to God.

Abram exchanged words of greeting with the visitor and explained what must be done if the man wished to enter the covenant with Yahweh. After listening intently, as each man before him had done, the visitor nodded his consent.

Abram picked up a skin flask of strong drink and held it out to the visitor, who eagerly took a long draft. Then the man disrobed.

"Here," said Abram holding out the leather handle of a whip. "Bite down onto this and hold tightly to the center pole of the tent."

Abram took the blade and began to cut the foreskin of his kins-man. The man flinched, groaned, and tightened every muscle. His teeth clenched. Tears streamed from his eyes and splattered into the coals of the fire with a hiss.

"There!" Abram exclaimed. "It is done."

Abram handed the man a small clay vessel of salve, and then a clean cloth in which to wrap himself. When he was finished dressing, the man looked into Abram's eyes, bowed once deeply, turned, and left the tent.

As Abram saw the tent flap close, he thought of the winding path-way that had brought him and his people to this time of commitment to their faith in Yahweh. It had been a long and difficult journey that had nearly broken his heart and that of his beloved Sarai. But now, after living nearly one hundred years, he was soon destined to become a father for the first time, and he recalled the events that led to this miraculous turn in their lives.

# — 1 —

He was born in an age when the archaic events of the great flood and the tower of Babel were still recalled around the fires as family stories, woven into the fabric that bound a desert people—the warp and weft of a lineage. The tree of Abram reached back for ten generations to Noah—Yahweh's hands—who had wrapped the living world inside an ark of wood from ancient cedars of Lebanon. Like those venerable trees, Abram's people had endured. His grandfather, Nahor, who survived for 119 journeys of the sun, had a boy named Terah. At the age of seventy, Terah fathered three sons: Abram, Nahor, and Haran.

Abram grew into a tall young man who was deeply reflective. After the rains had passed and the dry season begun, when other children played in the clay beds of the wadi, Abram took long walks into the hills. He came home to tell of watching a golden eagle prey on a coney, of seeing a kite swoop down and snatch a thrush in midair, or of studying the graceful motion of a crane as it stalked the marshes along the shore of the River Jordan. Always he looked beyond where others could see, as if searching for a glimpse into some distant future.

One day, Abram returned from a long sojourn, and his father could see that he was excited.

"Son," asked Terah, "what have you seen?"

"Father, I saw the most beautiful creature."

"What now?" asked his father. "A butterfly, a quail, a turtledove?"

Abram replied, "As soon as I saw her, my heart was bound. I fear I will never want anything as much as this young woman."

"Ah, I see," said Terah. "And her name?"

"She is called Sarai."

Abram's courtship of Sarai was brief and intense. His entire being was set on convincing her of the wisdom of their match.

"Who is this strange young man, so tall and serious?" Sarai's mother asked after the first time she met Abram.

"He is the son of Terah," Sarai replied. "Do you think he is handsome?"

"The question, daughter, is not what I think, but what your heart says when it speaks to you."

"There is something between us," she replied. "He, too, is young, yet he has an old soul. There is comfort in that. Yet there is something unsettling as well. The other day, as we sat under an almond tree in the orchard, he offered me a tea of cinnamon bark, which he had brought in his skin flask. We sipped from two cups of ram's horn. The scent of that tea … well … I have never tasted anything so delicious! I think it was spiced with a touch of cumin. Then, as we sat and drank, for the first time since we met, Abram spoke freely."

"What did he have to say?" asked Sarai's mother.

"He spoke of his admiration for the beauty of nature, for the white and yellow blooms of the rose of Sharon, the aromatic scent of the bay tree leaves during the heat of the dry season, of watching the purple water hen out on the marshes."

"And you?"

"I told him of my favorite bird—the ring dove. And mother, just as I said the bird's name, a dove began calling from a tree nearby! We looked at each other without speaking. It must have been a sign! Did you know that ring doves choose a partner and remain loyal to one another all their lives? Then we watched a scorpion creep onto a rock a short distance away and prey on a locust that very moment."

"And what was that a sign of?" asked Sarai's mother with a smile.

Sarai turned and looked at the woman and said sharply, "Mother, please!"

"Go on, go on then!" her mother implored.

"Then Abram said to me, 'This is the way of all Yahweh's creatures. That one will feed the other and nothing goes to waste.'"

"And … ?"

"He is handsome. He is wise and …"

"But Sarai, do you enjoy his company?"

"Very much, Mother."

"Ah, so …"

"It is not for me to decide."

"We shall see."

The day dawned clear and cool. A scent of jasmine floated down from the wedding tent where Sarai's family prepared the fragrant bundles, brewed the special teas, and opened the best wines.

"Mother, it is beautiful!" said Sarai as she saw the white linen dress with its fringed sash and matching necklace of ivory inlaid with jewels.

"It was my wedding dress and my mother's before," she replied as her eyes began to glisten. "Now Sarai, pull down the veil."

"Abram, you look splendid," said Terah.

"But, father, the cloth is so heavy. In the heat of the day I am going to sweat."

"Nonsense! That robe was made of cloth to mirror the hue of the rising sun. It is a symbol of new love and the fire of life. Nahor, Haran—each of you take hold of a handle and carry this urn of the groom's wine up to the wedding tent. Walk just behind us as we enter."

"Only if we get some to drink!" said Haran.

"Yes, yes, of course, in due time," answered Terah. "This is a celebration. Yahweh will smile upon us all today!"

As the two brothers trundled along with the heavy vessel of wine between them, Nahor said, "I'm smiling already just thinking about this wine."

"And the young women who will be arriving soon," added Haran.

"Yes, Brother. Many have been unveiled by a chalice of wine. And I ought to know."

"Nahor, I see that you have become a prophet."

"What do you mean?" asked Nahor.

"You speak convincingly about things that have yet to happen."

The vows were brief. Abram and Sarai were barely aware of what was said by the high priest; their eyes and ears were only for each other. At last, when the two lovers heard the words, "... with Yahweh as your witness," Abram lifted Sarai's veil and kissed her for the first time.

The feast and the music were as intoxicating as the night air. As the sun was setting, Sarai and Abram stole away from the crowd and wandered into an olive grove. Abram nervously caressed the smooth bark of an old tree.

"What a sky!" said Sarai.

"Perhaps the stars are a sign of the blessings we will share."

Abram placed his hand under Sarai's chin, slowly tilting her face upward, and pulled her close. He kissed her gently.

"You are beautiful," whispered Abram as Sarai stared silently into his eyes.

Abram stood up, took Sarai's hand, and helped her to her feet.

"Come with me, my wife. They have prepared a place for us."

Abram led Sarai from the olive grove and found a path that was lined with lit torches. After a short walk, they came to a small clearing in which stood a peaked tent, adorned with colorful ribbons that rustled in the breeze.

Together, they brushed passed the cloth door and stepped inside, greeted by the scent of myrrh, the incense of passion. The floor was covered with a rug woven of brightly colored wool. Soon they were lost in a dance that stopped time and transcended place.

# — 2 —

Months passed in the house of Sarai and Abram, a time of hope and anticipation. But Sarai did not become pregnant. They prayed, consulted a midwife, tried conceiving at every possible time during Sarai's moons.

Abram and Sarai embarked on a far-reaching journey. They moved northwest up the valley of the River Euphrates, then turned west to the distant shore of the Great Sea. There they visited the city of Dor, made their way south across the open expanse of the Plain of Sharon to Joppa, and then on to Gaza. Traveling in the cool of the mornings and evenings, they spent the heat of each day swimming in the Great Sea, visiting the small fishing villages, looking out over the marshes, and inhaling the earthy scents of the mudflats. They were inspired by the patience with which an egret would wait, motionless, for its moment to strike; marveled at how the groups of pelicans worked their powerful wings in tandem as they skimmed the water, inches above the waves; appreciated the graceful strength of the swans; awoke to the varied voices of hidden shorebirds, sounds that were stretched and softened by the wind.

In the quiet inlets and secluded islands hidden by tall grass where rivers flowed into the sea, Abram was mesmerized and, at times, overwhelmed by Sarai's beauty. Birds called from nearby trees, and the breeze caressed their skin and bent the reeds overhead and they felt inseparable from the timeless rhythms of the wind and the sea.

---

A year crept by, but nothing changed. One evening, Sarai came to Abram in tears. "I am sorry that I have not given us a child."

"We must be patient," said Abram. "Yahweh will not abandon our hopes."

A second year passed, and then another. Still, no child came.

The years gathered behind them like the crests of dunes. Abram's brother Haran married and his wife bore a daughter, whom they named Milcah. In time, Abram's other brother, Nahor, one day married Milcah. Haran fathered a son and named him Lot. When Lot grew up and married, his wife bore a daughter, whom they also named Milcah, and a son, Iscah. To Abram and Sarai, it seemed that life itself was moving forward without them.

"Have faith," Abram would say when they broached the subject. But he, too, was unsure. He felt as if he were riding a wild stallion with no reins to guide it, only the flowing mane in hand as he was carried swiftly toward the unknown.

Terah was a proud grandfather. Despite his many responsibilities as elder, he devoted much of his time to teaching and playing with the youngest members of his household.

One day, a slave came rushing into Terah's tent as he was giving lessons to Milcah and Iscah.

"Master," she cried, "Haran has taken grievously ill and his condition is dire. Come, follow me."

Terah hurried as fast as his aged legs would allow. He found Haran shivering with fever, even in the heat of the desert summer. Terah ordered that Haran be undressed and poultices laid upon his head, abdomen, and groin. But the fever was too far advanced. Within two days' time, Haran's breathing had slowed to occasional heaves of his chest. Then, he lay still.

"My son, my dear boy!" cried Terah in anguish.

The next morning, Terah looked into the still waters of the well and saw in the wrinkles of his face the very lines of the folded hills of his homeland. Terah still lived in Ur of the Chaldaeans, in lower Mesopotamia, the place where he was born and raised, along with his sons and daughters, and now his grandchildren. But the old familiar places that once comforted and tied him to his past now only reminded of Haran.

Some weeks later, Terah gathered together Abram and Sarai and his grandson Lot, the son of Haran.

"My time in these hills and fields, these olive groves and pastures, has come to an end. Once sweet as the date, my days are now bitter as the mandrake and filled with remorse. Please come with me to Canaan."

The next day, they set off by camel and ass: Terah, Sarai and Abram, Lot and his family, their slaves and servants, and all their worldly possessions. They traveled to the north and west of Mesopotamia. On the way to Canaan, they reached a beautiful valley and settled there.

Terah said, "I shall name this place after Haran."

They lived for many years in the land of Haran. When Terah's time was at hand, he passed quietly in the night at the age of two hundred and five.

— **3** —

One morning, soon after Abram had reached his seventy-fifth year, he went out into the desert to hunt roebuck. He walked to a sheltered grove of cedars of Lebanon, close to where he had seen a small herd of deer a few days earlier. Some of the majestic trees had a girth as wide as Abram was tall.

As he sat in silence, waiting, Yahweh spoke to him.

"Abram, your time in Haran has come to an end. Leave your father's house and his family. Your destiny lies in a new land."

"Thank you, God. This has become a place of sadness that conjures the face of a child who was never born."

"Blessed are you and Sarai, for your family is the root of the tree I will grow. One day, your name will be spoken as a blessing, and seeds from the fruit of that tree will sprout across the land."

Without delay, Abram gathered his wife Sarai and his nephew Lot, everything they owned, including their slaves and servants, and left on the journey to Canaan.

Some days into the journey, they entered the rich hinterlands of the Canaanites surrounding the holy site of Shechem. An ancient and magnificent tree grew there: the Oak of Moreh.

As they walked passed it, Abram inquired, "Sarai, do you see what that tree is telling us?"

In frustration, Sarai said, "First you ask us to leave our home for a new land with barely enough time to pack. Now you are saying that trees speak to you?"

"Not in words, but in symbols," said Abram.

"Husband, I trust in your faith, and I believe in your visions of Yahweh. But sometimes I wonder if the desert sun hasn't gone to your head."

They camped nearby for the night. After the evening meal, Abram walked by starlight to the ancient tree. He sat down and leaned back against its massive trunk. A breeze rustled the leaves overhead. As Abram listened, the sound of the wind through the branches began to form words that he could understand. Abram bowed down and listened.

"Abram, one day this land will nourish the scion of your family," said Yahweh. "The roots and branches will weigh heavy with flowers and fruit."

The next morning, Abram returned to the Oak of Moreh and raised an altar of stone. He went back to camp to get Sarai, and they led the group into the mountains that lay west of Ai.

That desolate land grew thorny, aromatic acacia trees, cassia, and spikenard, with its pungent leaves. In one sheltered oasis, they discovered the blooms of scarlet martagon—the red Turk's cap lily—and a small patch of the heavily scented mandrake, or *dudaim*. Here they raised their tent. Abram arranged stones to form an altar and offered prayers of thanks to Yahweh.

That evening, the great horned owl called to them. From a distant patch of lowland forest, the mournful notes of a cuckoo serenaded their meal. Ravens greeted them at dawn.

"Have you heard those birds calling to us?" Abram asked Sarai.

"Do I want to hear what they are saying?"

"They say we are getting close to our new home," he replied.

"I suppose if we, too, had wings, Abram, we *would* be close."

In this way, over many legs of a long journey, Abram and his family gradually neared the heart of Canaan.

Soon after they had settled to the south in the Negeb, a drought caused the crops to fail and a famine spread across the land.

"We cannot grow food in this parched soil," said Sarai. "Our stores will soon run out. Then what are we going to eat?"

"If we go down into Egypt we will be able to find enough food. They trade for food that is grown far away, in places where the rains still come."

"Then we should go," Sarai agreed.

"But I am worried," said Abram.

"Of what?"

"Of Pharaoh, the second Amenemhet, son of Senusret—he has never seen a woman of your beauty."

"But Abram ..."

"Let me finish. When Pharaoh meets you and sees the large number of people we bring with our family who all need to be provided for, he will ask to have you as his wife."

"That cannot be," Sarai insisted.

"Please, Sarai, listen to what I have to say. If Amenemhet wants you for his own, and he sees that I am your husband, he will surely have me killed."

"What are you saying we should do?"

"We should go to Egypt as sister and brother. Then, when Amenemhet hopes for you to be his wife, he will offer us food, shelter, and gifts."

Sarai's face hardened, and her stare grew cold. "I will not do this. There must be some other way."

"My dear wife, this may be the only way we can survive. Still, the sacrifice will be yours to accept or deny."

Sarai stood up and walked off along the familiar trails that led from their tent and out toward the well. She leaned over and stared down at her reflection. "This so-called blessing of beauty is a curse!" she thought to herself. Then she began to cry, and tears dripped into the placid waters, dimpling the surface and causing her reflection to dance and ripple. "That is the face of my future," Sarai thought. "What will I feel when I look back at the choice I must make today?"

By evening light, Sarai reappeared, walking up the trail. Abram was waiting. He watched her graceful steps, the fluid movement of her hips. "Yahweh has truly blessed me with such a wife," he thought.

Sarai sat down next to him, took his hand in hers, looked into his eyes, and wept.

Abram brought his family down into Egypt. Having heard that a powerful and important clan was coming to the city, Pharaoh Amenemhet arranged for a formal welcome at the gates. Abram and Sarai were ushered into the presence of Amenemhet.

As was custom, Abram greeted Pharaoh with a bow. When Amenemhet rose to offer Abram a formal embrace, his eyes looked over the shoulder of the tall, dark man before him. Amenemhet's breath caught at the sight of Sarai, whose eyes were cast downward. "Such sadness in those eyes," he thought.

Stepping aside, Abram said, "And here is my sister, Sarai."

Amenemhet nodded to Sarai, and she proffered a slight bow.

That same night, a messenger came to Abram and asked for Sarai to join Amenemhet as his wife. Abram accepted the offer.

Sarai followed the messenger into an ornate chamber that was decorated with gold filigree and velvet tapestries. In the center was a large bed shrouded in fine drapes. A servant led Sarai to the bed and drew back the hangings. She saw that Amenemhet was waiting. His body glistened with an oil of a fragrance alien to Sarai. Lying in Amenemhet's room, Sarai found herself drifting, once again walking the trails through the hills of her youth, listening to the familiar birds, and drinking from her family's well. She saw the face of her mother and father as she entered their tent after a long walk and felt their sweet embrace. She would take this same walk many times during her family's stay in Egypt.

In the days that followed, as drought and famine continued to ravage the countryside, Amenemhet treated Abram's clan generously. They were given as much fowl as they could eat. Camels and donkeys were led into their stables as gifts. Offerings of new slaves, both men and women, also came to Abram.

Yahweh saw all these things and was enraged.

———

"Master," pleaded one of Pharaoh's slaves, "your eldest daughter has become gravely sick during the night."

"How could this have happened without forewarning? I will go to her," said Pharaoh.

"She is not the only one taken ill," said the slave. "Throughout the city people are stricken and many are dying."

Amenemhet found his beloved daughter upon her deathbed. In a blur of tears, he turned to his counsel and asked, "What have our people done to bring this upon our city?"

"Master, may I speak truly?"

"Yes."

"It is said that your new wife is not Abram's sister."

"What is she then?"

"Please be kind, master," said the slave. "I only bear the news."

"Speak!"

"It is rumored that Sarai is Abram's wife."

"Summon them both at once!" cried Amenemhet.

When Abram and Sarai arrived at Amenemhet's private chambers, he was pacing. As they entered, Amenemhet reached out, grabbed Sarai by the arm, and pulled her toward him.

"Are these rumors true?" he demanded.

"Yes," Abram admitted. "Sarai is my wife."

"I took Sarai as *my* wife because of your deceit!" Amenemhet bellowed. "How could I have known? You told me that Sarai was your sister. Your cunning has brought a plague upon my family and my people."

Amenemhet pushed Sarai toward Abram so hard that she fell to the stone floor. "Leave this place and never return. Both of you—go!"

Pharaoh's men waited as Abram, Lot, and Sarai prepared to leave, along with their slaves. Later that same day they left Egypt for the Negeb, plodding slowly across the desert with herds of goats, livestock, fowl, and camels laden with their belongings sacks straining with silver and gold. But that weight could not compare with the heaviness in their hearts, burdened by acts of betrayal and shame in the eyes of God.

# — 4 —

Many days passed as they traveled the rough trails that led toward the mountains to the place that lay north and west of beth El and Ai—the land of the Canaanites and the Perizzites. Not once did Sarai look at her husband, or allow him to touch her. The rains had returned; the land was lush in the lowlands and along the shores. But the verge of sunlit green could not warm the ice Sarai felt in her heart. Abram, however, endured the heat of shame, a burning that was stoked by the fuel of Sarai's silence and distance.

They found their homeland green and growing. The fields, although unkempt, could be planted with wheat, rye, barley, millet, and flax. Gardens around the tents would again be fragrant with the scents of anise, coriander, and black cumin.

Soon after their return, when the settlement was organized and productive, Abram climbed to the place where he had built an altar some years before. The stones were as he had left them.

"Yahweh, that my faith might be as these stones—steadfast and lasting. But the world is a hard and dangerous place. The winds of recent events have bent my will to their whims, and I have strayed from your path."

Yahweh was silent. Abram stood, alone with his thoughts and with a confused heart.

Down in the lowlands, the kinsmen of Abram and Lot tended their flocks of sheep and herds of cattle. But there were many animals, and the land could not feed them all. The herdsmen began to argue and fight about who would take the best grazing land in that valley.

When Abram heard this, he went to visit his nephew, Lot. "Come, let us walk," he said.

With Lot at his side, Abram asked, "Why should we fight? Our families spring from the same tree. This land is big enough for us both."

They climbed into the nearby hills. Abram gestured out toward the expanse of fertile land before them. "Yahweh has been generous to us. Choose the place where you would make your home, east or west, and my family will live in the lands that remain."

A fertile plain lay to the east. Lot saw there a rich land fed by canals bringing water from the River Jordan. This vast garden stretched as far as the land of Zoar, on the southern shores of the Sea of Arabah.

"There," said Lot, pointing to the south and east. "That is where I choose to live with my people. In the land surrounding the city of Sodom." Though the land was good and the life of a wealthy herdsman would be easy in that place, Lot also knew that thieves roamed the region. Armed with swords, they raided farms and villages, hurting innocent people and raising the ire of Yahweh.

Again Abram led his family away to the west, to the land of Canaan.

On the day they arrived, Sarai discovered an oasis. Years ago, someone had planted date palms and fig trees in the dark soil.

"This is where we will build a home," she told Abram. "Here I am going to plant almond and myrtle and olive trees; carob, cinnamon, and hyssop. Rose of Sharon will go over there!"

These were the first words Sarai had spoken to Abram since they fled the household of Pharaoh. He watched her and was swept up in the excitement of settling in that place for a time.

"Yes," said Abram, "and over here we can plant pistachio and pomegranate!"

Then their eyes met with the warmth of old. Abram stepped toward Sarai and gently placed his arms around her. He ran his fingers along her shoulders and drew her close. Sarai's arms remained at her side, but she slowly let her head fall until it rested against Abram's chest.

That evening Sarai and Abram walked into the hills and radiated in the glow of the late day sun. As they stood in silence and content, Yahweh spoke to them.

"Behold this land, as far as you can see—south toward Moriah and on to the Negeb. Look east to the hill country and beyond where the Salt Sea glistens in the sun. In this land your house will grow until your descendants are as many as the grains of sand. Walk on this earth. See its beauty with your own eyes, smell the scent of the leaves on the walnut tree, listen to the cry of the falcon. These, too, will be your kin."

After wandering for a time in that land, Sarai and Abram settled in Hebron. In his gratitude for the gifts bestowed by Yahweh, Abram built an altar beneath the branches of the Oak of Mamre and offered prayers of thanks. On many walks they returned to the oasis that had been the gateway to that land, each time bringing some new seed of a beloved flower or seedling of a favorite tree, adding to their secret Eden and nurturing the tender shoots of forgiveness.

## — 5 —

After they had lived in Hebron for some time, a haggard, beaten soldier came into Abram's tent at the Oak of the Amorite Mamre.

"Master," he said, "Sodom and Gomorrah have been defeated by the armies of King Chedor-laomer and his allies. The cities have been sacked."

Abram seized the messenger and drew him close, his breath hot on the soldier's face.

"And what of my nephew, Lot, who was living in Sodom?" he demanded.

"He and his family have been taken with the others," the soldier replied.

Abram sounded the alarm and gathered more than three hundred of his kinsmen, who sharpened swords and strung bows to prepare for battle. They set out in force and soon picked up the trail of the invading army. Abram's men pursued them far to the north until they reached the city of Dan. There they lay in wait and watched in the waning light.

Abram's forces attacked at nightfall. Although they had the advantage of surprise, the invaders had remained on guard. The battle was close, brutal, and bloody. Men cried out as the edge of a sword or point of an arrow found its mark. The eerie stillness of the night was rent by the sounds of clashing metal and the groans of the wounded. When the blood moon rose, it shone down on a battlefield littered with broken bodies.

Overpowered, the invaders fled to the northeast, beyond Damascus and on to the city of Hobah, where they were pursued and finally defeated by Abram and his men.

Abram searched through the tents in the enemy's camp. Some were cut to shreds, others were burning. In one large tent he found his nephew, Lot, and many of Lot's people, bound and gagged. He untied Lot and embraced him.

"I feared that I would not see you again," said Abram.

"Uncle, you are our savior," said Lot. "Praise Yahweh!"

"Sometimes Yahweh looks after those who fight their own battles," said Abram.

The rest of Lot's kinfolk were found unharmed nearby, and all their goods were recovered.

When Abram and his kinsmen returned to the Valley of Shaveh, they were greeted by the high priest Melchizedek.

"I give you bread and wine to mark this victory. On this day, the house of Abram is blessed by the Creator, the most high God, who has given you and your kinsmen the strength to defeat your enemies."

That night, by the fire of his kinsmen, the wine flowed freely. As the evening grew old, long silences befell the weary soldiers. After the children were asleep, some of the wives came to join the fire ring.

During one long silence, Lot's wife said, "Here is a story that was told to me by a merchant's wife, who had heard it in the city of the pharaoh. She began this way: '*Kan ma kan. Bidaa nihki, willa innam.*'"

"What does that mean in our tongue?" asked one of the soldiers.

Lot's wife replied, "There was, there was not. Shall we tell stories, or sleep on our cots?"

After the laughter died down, she began her tale.

Abu l'Hssein, the Fox, was trotting along a trail one day, when he saw Raven perched in a tree. "Friend, Raven," called Abu l'Hssein, "would you like to come and visit me? I will give you something good to eat."

"Yes, I would like that," replied Raven.

"Meet me at the rock in front of my den this evening," said Abu l'Hssein as he loped toward home. Once he arrived at his den, Abu l'Hssein began to prepare a meal of porridge for Raven. First he put some camel's milk in a pot and boiled it slowly over the fire. When the milk was ready, he mixed in some flour and stirred until it thickened.

Raven soon flew in and landed near Abu l'Hssein.

"Hello," said Abu l'Hssein.

"What are you making?" asked Raven.

"Dinner," replied Abu l'Hssein. Raven, who was very hungry, watched as his friend prepared the meal.

Once the porridge was done, Abu l'Hssein poured it out onto the flat rock on which he was standing. "Here is our meal," he said. "Eat well, my friend."

Raven pecked and pecked at the porridge, but was barely able to eat a tiny morsel. The longer he tried, the more frustrated and hungry he became. Meanwhile, Abu l'Hssein lapped up the porridge until his belly was full.

"This foolish Abu l'Hssein," thought Raven, "what kind of friend is he? I cannot eat this way!"

"Abu l'Hssein," said Raven in the most friendly manner he could manage, "you have been most kind and generous by inviting me for this fine meal. Please allow me to repay the favor and prepare a feast for you. I will provide as many sweet dates as you can possibly eat!"

Since sweet dates were Abu l'Hssein's favorite food, he became very excited. "Absolutely!" he cried. "Those dates grow so high in the date palms that I can only eat the few that fall on the ground and don't get consumed before I happen to find them."

"Excellent," answered Raven. "Meet me at the base of my tree tomorrow at sunset." Raven then flew toward home.

Abu l'Hssein arrived the following evening just as the sun was dipping below the distant hills. He saw his friend, Raven, up in the date palm tree, silhouetted against the orange glow of a beautiful evening sky.

"I am going to knock these dates down for you to eat," Raven called down to Abu l'Hssein. "Get ready to catch them." Raven started picking the sweet dates. But, instead of knocking them down where Abu l'Hssein could reach them, he dropped them into the middle of a dense thorn bush.

Abu l'Hssein ran in circles around the thorn bush in search of a way in. But, no matter how hard he tried, Abu l'Hssein could not reach through the thorns to get the dates. In a short time, his snout was cut up, his lips were red and swollen, and his paws were raw and bleeding from reaching into the thorns.

Raven flew down from the tree. He used his hard beak and scaly claws to pluck one date after another from amid the tangle of thorns. Soon, he had eaten his fill. Raven sat back against the base of the date palm, wrapped his wings around his middle, and groaned with delight.

At that moment, Abu l'Hssein realized what Raven had been doing. Instead of looking upon his friend as an inferior, Abu l'Hssein now regarded Raven as an equal. Abu l'Hssein developed a deep respect for his friend. He realized that, although Raven's ways were different than his own, they worked just as well to help him survive.

# — 6 —

Sarai constantly watched for signs that she had conceived. Every cycle of the moon brought expectation, followed by disappointment. Each year the cord of grief tightened around her heart as the light of hope faded in the gray skies of age.

One evening, as they sat by the cooking fire, Sarai said heavily to Abram, "Again the moon is gone and I am without child. The years are mounting like drifts of sand. My heart can no longer bear this burden. I fear we are being punished for our sins in Egypt. Is this the price we must pay for our lives, for our wealth, and for our land?"

The unfulfilled dream of their deepest desire lay before them—a future that sometimes appeared as withered and lifeless as a wadi in the height of the dry season.

During the next few days, Abram trekked far to the south and eventually climbed the peak of Har Dimona. That night, under a moonless desert sky awash with stars, Abram prayed.

"Yahweh, Lord, how can we go on?"

In the early hours of the morning Abram grew tired. He rested his head on his breast and closed his eyes.

"All these years I have protected you," spoke Yahweh. "Do not be afraid. Your time will soon be at hand."

"Are you to give us an heir, or must one of my kinsmen inherit my title and land?" asked Abram.

"No, that will not come to pass. Your own flesh and blood will inherit the fruits of your life with Sarai."

"How can that be?"

"Look to the sky," said Yahweh. "How many stars do you see?"

"So many that I cannot possibly count them," Abram replied.

"Your descendants will be as many as these."

At that moment, Abram's faith was restored, and Yahweh found him worthy.

"Now," said Yahweh, "I was the one who delivered you and Sarai to your homeland many years ago."

Abram listened as the shadow of an owl slipped across the moon.

"Bring me a ram, a goat, and a heifer, being all of three years old. Also a turtledove and a squab."

Abram went out into the night to find his flocks and dovecotes. By the end of the next day he returned with a cart bearing the carcasses of the animals and birds. Abram split the three animals and arrayed the half of each across from the other. Blood oozed and soaked into the hot, dry sand. Griffon vultures swooped down and tried to feed, but Abram waved his arms and yelled to drive them away.

A glow began to blush on the horizon. Weary, Abram lay down and slept. But his dreams were dark, and he awoke shivering in the cool evening air, filled with loneliness and dread.

"Fear not, Abram," Yahweh comforted, "for I am here. One day, like stars enshrouded by clouds, your multitude of descendants will be enslaved and made to do the bidding of others in a foreign land."

"How long?" asked Abram tremulously.

"Four hundred years," Yahweh replied.

Abram's head fell hard against his chest. Tears flowed freely as he pictured the suffering of his heirs. He tore his shirt in anguish, screaming, "Why!"

"At the end of that time," Yahweh continued, "your heirs will be freed, a wealthy people. When your own time comes, you will join those of your house who have gone before you, fulfilling your destiny and with peace in your heart."

Abram waited and witnessed in silence as night settled on steady wings. He closed his eyes and tried to imagine the future that Yahweh had set before him.

Then, through his eyelids, Abram saw a red glow and began to feel heat. A fire was burning on the sands, but with no fuel to feed the lapping flames. With a sudden roar, tongues of flame shot out and flowed as liquid fire between the halves of the slaughtered animals. Abram raised his arm to shield his face and cowered, crying out, "Here is the hand of Yahweh before me!"

"This is my covenant with you, Abram. Your heirs will inherit the great verge of land from the River Euphrates and down to Egypt, to the Wadi al'Arish," Yahweh promised in a voice that made the mountaintop tremble.

— 7 —

Like the spiraling leaves of an artichoke, the years unfolded. Still Sarai conceived no child. In those days, in the land of Mesopotamia, if a married couple could not bear children, the wife could choose to have a female slave conceive in her place.

One day, Sarai approached Abram. "Husband, I have accepted my fate. I can see only one way that we will ever have an heir."

"And how is that, Sarai?"

"An Egyptian slave girl named Hagar lives with our people. Would you consent to have her bear your child?"

After a lengthy consideration, Abram agreed to the arrangement.

In the time marked by less than the turn of a moon, Hagar discovered that she was expecting a child. She also found, to her delight, that this privilege bestowed upon her a certain standing among the kin of Abram and Sarai. Unaccustomed to such honor, Hagar soon began to swell with self-importance. She treated Sarai with disrespect and even disdain.

"See what you have done!" Sarai said to Abram. "Hagar has become blind to her true place. She treats me as an equal … no … as if she is above me."

"Do with her what you will," said Abram, seeing no other recourse.

Sarai began to return Hagar's insults and her attitude, giving the slave girl the most menial tasks and taking every opportunity to remind her of her subservience.

Hagar soon despaired and fled the house of Abram and Sarai. Wandering into the desert along the road to Shur, somewhere between Bered and Kadesh, Hagar discovered a well. As she dipped some water to drink, the most beautiful face she had ever seen appeared in place of her reflection.

"Hagar," came a voice, "I can see that you are lost. The path that has led you to this place is rocky and the road ahead uncertain."

"Who are you?" asked Hagar.

"I am an angel sent by Yahweh to guide you."

"My mistress is cruel. I feared that my own anger would lead me to harm her if I did not leave."

"Sarai is blinded by jealousy and grief," said the angel. "Still, your rightful place is in her house. Endure Sarai's insults, and you will be rewarded with a son."

"What of this son?"

"He will be the first branch of your tree, which will bear fruit as abundant as your wildest dreams. He will have the temperament of a wild animal. His life will be a struggle to gain Yahweh's attention. He will fight everyone, especially those he is closest to, including his brothers. You will name him Ishmael, 'hear me God.'"

"As surely as I have seen you in this well, and you have looked into my future, you are the voice of Yahweh. I will call this place Lahai Roi, 'the well of the seeing spirit.'"

Hagar returned to the house of Sarai. Abram was in his eighty-sixth year when Ishmael was born.

When Ishmael was beginning adolescence, Abram went off into the desert to be alone. There, Yahweh spoke to him.

"I am El Shaddai, the God who came to you on the mountain."

Abram lowered his head in shame and anguish. "You have witnessed my life. You have seen how I gave my wife to the pharaoh, how I bore a child with Hagar. I am not worthy."

Yahweh replied, "Abram, by your faith, your wrongs have been forgiven. I have watched you struggle with hardship through many long years, yet, in your heart, you have remained true to me. In time you and Sarai will become a great tree whose branches will bear countless flowers and fruit. Your descendants will number as the stars. No longer will your name be Abram. I give you to the future, *ab hamon,* 'father of millions.' Now you are Abraham.

"This is my covenant to you, Abraham, and to all of your descendants. All the lands of Canaan shall be yours forever. Your heirs will become nations and kings. And I shall be your God, without end."

"What would you have me do?" asked Abraham.

"Many years ago, I gave your forebear, Noah, the sign of the rainbow as a mark of my covenant. Now, you will bear a new symbol of the bond that encircles your heart. Circumcise yourself and decree that all your descendants will be circumcised as a mark of our covenant."

"As men?" asked Abraham

"When each child is eight days old," answered Yahweh.

"And what of those who are men now, or who join with us as men?"

"They, too, shall be circumcised."

"Sarai will now be named Sarah, for she is truly a princess. Your son by Sarah will begin the lineage of kings and queens."

"What are you saying?"

"Your hope has faded, but your faith has remained strong. My blessing will be the son that Sarah will bear."

Overwhelmed with joy, Abraham sank to the ground on his knees. His laughter burst a dam of grief, and a stream flowed from his eyes until his beard was soaked with tears of joy. Abraham shook with spasms of elation. Then he gradually fell silent as doubt caused him to fear that he had misunderstood.

"How may a husband and wife, whose age is the sum of nearly two hundred years, conceive a child? Surely you must mean Ishmael, who is now a young man of thirteen years."

"I will also enter a covenant with Ishmael, whose lineage shall bear witness to twelve generations. But Abraham, be assured, I speak now of Sarah's blood. She will bear a son before the next year has passed. And you will name him Isaac, 'God has smiled.'"

With those words of promise and with dreams still singing in his ears, Abraham looked around and realized that Yahweh was gone.

Abraham rushed downhill to his family. He gathered Ishmael and all the other men. They sat quietly as Abraham told them of the visit from Yahweh and of the covenant with the house of Abraham.

Then Abraham sharpened his knife and burnished the edge in the flames of the cooking fire until it was clean. He retired to his tent, and there built another small fire. First Ishmael and then each of the men went in, and Abraham circumcised them all.

When this was finished, Abraham summoned Sarah into the tent. He turned the knife in his hand, gripped the blade lightly and gestured to Sarah that she should take hold of the handle.

"But I do not know what to do!" she protested.

"I will guide you," said Abraham.

# — 8 —

One day, soon after the circumcisions had healed, the heat became almost unbearable. Abraham pulled his cloak over his head and sought shelter in front of his tent in the shade beneath the Oak of Mamre. After some time had passed, Abraham noticed a bit of dust rising and heard the rustle of garments. When he pulled back his hood and looked up, Abraham saw three men standing before him.

"Please," said Abraham bowing to the strangers in a gesture of respect and friendship. "Come cool yourself here in the shade. Your feet will be washed and a meal brought to restore you for the rest of your journey. If you are pleased, perhaps you will stay with us for a time and visit my family."

"Thank you," said one.

"As you wish," replied another.

"So be it," said the third and tallest among them.

At that moment, the veil was lifted from Abraham's eyes.

"Honor," he asked, "we have met before, have we not?"

"Yes, Abraham," replied the most commanding of the three.

Abraham now realized who the visitors were. He hurried off and gathered three bushels of flour. These he brought to Sarah and asked her to knead the flour into bread. Abraham slaughtered his finest calf and had his servant prepare it. When the bread and meat were ready to eat, they were laid out on a table with milk and cream beneath the Oak of Mamre. The three visitors stood and ate.

"Is your wife going to join us?" asked the guest.

"If you wish," replied Abraham. "She is there, in the tent."

Once he knew that Sarah could hear him, the tallest guest continued.

"A year from now, when I return, we will again share a meal beneath this ancient tree. Together we will celebrate the birth of your newborn son."

"What!" gasped Sarah beneath her breath from where she stood listening just inside the tent. She was beside herself that a stranger, of all people, would presume such a thing. "I am an elder who long ago stopped observing her moons," she thought, as one whose constant companion was the withered hope of a child that never came.

Sarah stepped out of the tent and stared at the tall visitor. She wondered to herself, "Will I, an old woman, and Abraham, an old man … will we enjoy our time together as we once did? And will a child come to us at this age?"

Imagining this, Sarah laughed out loud.

"Abraham," asked the visitor, "why did Sarah laugh at the thought of having a child? Does she not believe that, with me, everything is possible?"

Hearing that the visitor had read her thoughts, Sarah's smile vanished and was replaced by a look of fear.

"Sir," said Sarah quietly, "I did not laugh at what you said. I … I must have been thinking of something else."

"No, you heard me," the visitor replied, "And you did laugh."

After they were done eating, Abraham agreed to guide Yahweh and his two companions to the town of Sodom.

"Why do you travel to Sodom?" asked Abraham.

"I have made you a leader of your lineage, to uphold the ways of living justly and to rule with mercy," Yahweh said. "Your people are blessed and will one day be among the great nations on Earth. Now, as a leader of a great people, there is something I must tell you. Have you heard of the heinous sins being committed by the peoples of Sodom and Gomorrah?"

"I have," answered Abraham.

"It grieves me to hear of the sins of those peoples, for they are so plentiful and vile that it breaks my heart."

"What will you do?" Abraham asked.

"My messengers will go into the city to be my eyes."

As Yahweh's two companions walked toward the city, Abraham stood at his side and watched them go. Their feet left no prints in the sand. Abraham could see a faint gossamer movement just behind their shoulders in the waning evening light, and then only with a sideways glance. At last Abraham saw their true selves. They were neither men nor messengers. They were angels of God. Abraham now understood the true purpose of their visit, and a shiver of fear ran through him.

"I do not mean to presume any wisdom next to yours, Lord, for I am just a few grains of sand in your great desert," said Abraham, "but surely you don't mean to destroy the entire city of Sodom just to punish those who have sinned. You are looked to as the ultimate source of justice. Think of all the innocent people. Even if there are only fifty honest people in the entire city who follow your laws, would you also kill them in order to punish the sinners?"

"No, I would spare the entire city if fifty of its citizens live justly," responded Yahweh.

"And what if only forty just citizens are discovered?"

"Then I would spare them all."

"How about thirty?"

"They would live."

"Please, Lord, do not be impatient with me. What if there are only twenty, or as few as ten just citizens?"

"The city would stand," Yahweh replied again.

Then Yahweh walked over a rise and was gone. Abraham slowly made his way home, burdened with a troubled heart and struggling with his notion of righteousness.

When the two angels reached the city of Sodom, they found Lot tending the gate.

"Greetings," said Lot. "You appear to be virtuous men, of whom there are few in this city. Please, come to my house. I can give you food and drink and a place to sleep for the night."

"No," replied one of the strangers. "That is not why we are here."

"Whatever your business, is," said Lot, "you will need to eat and rest."

"We think not …"

"Come, come …," said Lot, gesturing down a narrow street.

Relenting, the two visitors followed Lot to his house. In silence, they ate a dinner of unleavened bread. Outside, news spread of the strange, handsome visitors, and a crowd of people gathered outside Lot's house.

"Send those men out to us," they yelled to Lot. "We want to abuse them."

Lot went to the door and opened it a crack. "No, they are my guests and you know the custom. They are due the privilege and safety of refuge here in this house."

"There is no standing on privilege left in this city!" cried one of the men. "Where have you been living these past years—in a sheep's blind?"

Seeing that there was no way to reason with the crowd, which could easily overpower him, Lot opened the door again and said, "Very well, but you cannot have the visitors. I offer my daughters instead, who are still in possession of their virtue."

But the men rushed the door, pushed Lot aside, and threw him to the ground. When the crowd tried to seize the two strangers, each of them stood up and rose to a tremendous height.

The two visitors bent down and said to Lot and his daughters in sonorous voices that shook the walls of the house, "Turn your eyes away!"

Then their countenance began to glow with a brilliant light and their robes became luminous. The attackers were compelled to stare as the light became as bright as the sun. In that instant, all of those in that room, save Lot and his daughters, were struck blind.

Addressing Lot, the two angels said, "Gather your wife and daughters and leave the city immediately. This evil place will soon be brought down by the wrath of Yahweh."

Lot and his wife and their two daughters gathered their belongings.

"There is no time," said the two visitors. "Flee now! Go up into the hills."

"Please, at least allow us to run to that small village in the distance," said Lot pointing to the south.

"Very well, but move quickly. Whatever you hear behind you, do not look back!" On into the night they ran, stumbling along the trail as the sounds of screaming and anguish rose up from the city of Sodom.

Just as the sun began to appear, Yahweh caused fire, rock, and ash to fall from the heavens, burying the cities Sodom and Gomorrah and all the surrounding villages. The land itself split open and swallowed the people where they stood.

Lot's wife tired of running. As she slowed down to rest, a large rock nearly landed on her. At that moment, she thought of her home and worried about the friends left behind in Sodom. Possessed with a great sense of loss, she began to turn her head back toward Sodom to see if the city was still standing.

Lot cried out, "No, *no,* do not look back!" But it was too late. As soon as Lot's wife turned her head, she was transformed into a pillar of salt.

In time, a strange silence came over the land. The skies cleared, and an eagle called overhead. Everyone who had lived in those places—women, children, and men—had been killed and entombed in a grave of heat and ash.

# — 9 —

At about the time that all of this occurred, Abraham, Sarah, and their people made a long journey west to the Negeb and settled in the land known as Gerar. As he had done many years before with Pharaoh, Abraham offered Sarah to Abimelech, King of Gerar, telling him that Sarah was his sister.

"Is this so?" asked Abimelech.

Sarah was silent.

That night, Sarah came to the tent of Abimelech while he was asleep. But before Abimelech lay with Sarah, Yahweh appeared to him in a dream.

"Sarah is Abraham's wife," said Yahweh. "If you yield to the temptation of sleeping with her, you and your people will be visited by a plague, and all will die."

"How could I have known?" asked Abimelech. "Abraham told me she was his sister!"

Yahweh spared the lives of Abimelech and his people because the king sent Sarah back to Abraham untouched. Then Yahweh made all the women of Abimelech's house barren.

"But Lord, I discovered the truth and resisted the temptation. Why did you punish my people?"

"You can go to the prophet Abraham and ask him to speak to me on your behalf."

"And why, Lord, is Abraham not punished for his sin?"

"It is a fair question, my son, and the answer is this: Abraham is one of the chosen."

Abimelech went to Abraham and said, "Why have you brought this sin upon my house?"

"I did it out of fear," said Abraham, "that you would murder me and steal my wife. And, truly, she is my half sister."

"How could this be?" asked Abimelech.

"Sarah is the daughter of my father, but not of my mother."

As Abimelech walked away, he thought, "Abraham's people may be blessed by God, but they are a strange lot." Still, he gave Abraham livestock and slaves and offered his people a place to stay wherever he chose to travel in his lands. He also gave Abraham one thousand pieces of silver as a token of honor for how Sarah was treated.

Then Abraham spoke to Yahweh in prayer, "Please, do not punish these good people for my own sin."

Yahweh replied, "So be it." At that moment, all the women in Abimelech's houses were again made whole and fertile.

Sarah and Abraham settled in that beautiful land. One day, a servant came to Abraham and said, "Master, some men have taken control of our well and will not allow anyone to gather water there."

"Who has done this?" asked Abraham.

"They are servants of Abimelech."

"Go and ask the king to meet me at the well at dusk," said Abraham.

Abraham went to the well as the sun was setting, where he found Abimelech and Phicol, the leader of his soldiers.

Abraham said, "This well was dug by my men. My people cannot live in this region without it."

"I do not know who would have turned people away from this water," responded Abimelech. "They certainly were not my men."

Abraham looked into the eyes of his erstwhile neighbor who was still their host in that land. He saw there a confirmation of why he suspected the well had been seized: King Abimelech sought a gesture acknowledging that the well lay within his domain.

"Here, then, are cattle and sheep," said Abraham as he led them to Abimelech. This gift sealed the agreement that Abraham's people should use the well.

"Here, too, are seven lambs, which I offer, that you will accept the rights of my people who dug this well."

Abimelech agreed, and from that day on, that place was called Beersheba, "well of the seven lambs."

After Abimelech departed with his troops, Abraham planted a willow there to honor Yahweh.

## — 10 —

One morning, Sarah came to Abraham and said, "Husband, I feel weak and faint on my feet. My stomach is churning."

"I told you not to drink that pomegranate wine last night. It doesn't agree with you."

"I don't think that's what it is."

"What are you telling me, Sarah?"

"After all of these long years, Yahweh has fulfilled his promise."

"You're not saying that ..."

"Yes, Abraham, my beloved husband," Sarah whispered as she put her arms around him and kissed his neck. "I am with child."

For Sarah and Abraham, the coming moons were a blur of days where every activity was merely a diversion while waiting for the birth of their child.

Then, on Abraham's one hundredth birthday, Sarah came to Abraham and said, "Husband, it is time!"

The labor was long and arduous. Many times the baby seemed about to crown, but then Sarah's tired body relaxed and the birthing slowed once more.

After hours of this exhausting rhythm, Sarah lay nearly in a stupor. One more time she felt the waves of imminent birth wash over her; again she pushed with every morsel of strength she possessed. This time, just as the child was beginning to move, Sarah heard the call of the ring dove wash over her from a nearby tree. Her heart and spirit and effort were renewed, and the baby crowned.

Shortly after that, the nursemaid placed a tiny bundle upon Sarah's breast. "Mistress," she said, "here is your son."

"I have never seen a more beautiful child!" Sarah exclaimed.

"Let us call him Isaac," said Abraham, "after the laughter and play he will bring into our lives."

Abraham circumcised Isaac when he was eight days old, as Yahweh had told him to do.

Sarah's days were filled with nursing and cleaning and simply being with her newborn. In all of the long, disappointing years that had led up to Isaac's birth, never had she imagined, or even dared to consider, that she could feel such joy and deep contentment as she did now with his tiny star guiding her life. Isaac's features reminded her of Abraham's face, even the promise of his aquiline nose. His eyes, however, recalled those of Sarah's mother, or, perhaps, even her own.

Some moons later, after Isaac was weaned, Abraham arranged for a feast and celebration. During the festivities, Sarah watched as Ishmael entertained his younger brother. She saw the children playing string games and noticed how the patterns were never predictable.

"That has been my life," she mused. "One twist of the wrist, a small crook in a finger, and the outcome is changed. A life governed by unwritten fates that are a mystery to all but Yahweh."

Sarah's heart was torn because she could see that Ishmael and Isaac were close and enjoyed each other's company. But she was determined that neither Ishmael nor Hagar would inherit any of the land and possessions of herself and Abraham.

That night, after the celebration, she told Abraham of her intent.

"But Ishmael is also my son," Abraham reminded her. "I do not want to become estranged from the boy over concern about property and inheritance. Let me think upon it."

That evening, Abraham walked out into the fields to where an old carob tree was growing, its branches lacy against the moonlit sky. A seedpod crunched beneath his feet and a sweet aroma wafted up.

"Lord," said Abraham, "my heart is torn between the wishes of my beloved and love for my firstborn son, Ishmael. What would you have me do?"

"Abraham, honor Sarah's wishes. She has suffered long, and her time for happiness has come."

"But what of Ishmael and *his* happiness?"

"I will provide for Ishmael. He will grow into a tree of his own, and I will cause the branches to spread forth and bear the abundant fruit of his heirs."

With a heavy heart, Abraham replied, "As you say, so it will be."

At daybreak, Abraham went to Hagar and told her of his wishes. "I cannot raise Isaac in a house divided."

Hagar's eyes blazed. "As soon as I learned of Sarah's pregnancy, I knew this day would come," she said with bitterness. "Sarah is too proud to bear the birth of her own true son next to Ishmael."

"I will see that you are given ample provisions," said Abraham. "They will last no matter how long your journey will take to settle in a new homeland. From this point on, we will walk separate paths."

Abraham reached out to Hagar, but she drew back. "I have to pack," she said. She turned to Ishmael. "Come," she said sharply, "we have work to do." Then she ushered him into their tent.

Hagar and Ishmael prepared to leave. They said goodbye to no one. Leading a camel and an ass loaded with food and other necessities, they set out across the desert wilderness. For two days they wandered until their supply of water ran out. In her despair, and not knowing how she would ever provide for Ishmael, Hagar abandoned him and ran out into the night. Some distance away, she sat down next to a large rock. There she finally wept the tears she had held in for all of Ishmael's childhood, tears that she would never have allowed anyone close to Abraham and his kinfolk to see.

Through her tears of anger, sadness, and despair, Hagar saw a strange being. "It must be a spirit," she thought. "No, I am just tired and hungry and parched. I am hallucinating."

"Hagar," said the angel, "your tears have touched Yahweh deeply, and your faith has been steadfast. One day, Ishmael will become the wellhead of a people who will grow as wide and deep as a great river."

Hagar stood up. She walked back toward Ishmael, taking the same path, and discovered a well from which to drink and fill her flask of hide with water. She stared at the well and wondered, "Did I pass this well earlier and not see it, or has it appeared where there was no well before?"

When she reached Ishmael she held the flask to his lips and he drank deeply.

Over the coming years Ishmael grew to manhood. He wandered the wilderness of Paran and became a hunter who was highly skilled with a bow. Ishmael's reputation as a man of strength and will grew into a legend. Some said he had the heart of a lion, others the courage of a badger. He could be brash and impetuous and wild, but was reputed a fair man who was always kind to children and inclined toward women. In time, Hagar found a wife for Ishmael in Egypt, and he began to raise a family of his own. As Yahweh had promised, Ishmael's family tree grew. Its branches began to spread throughout that land. But unrest and anger continued to burn in Ishmael's heart, stoked by the glowing embers of injustice.

Isaac grew quickly in the eyes of Sarah and Abraham. Although they were both of great age, Isaac brought the joys of youth into their lives, healing the lonely scars of childless years.

One day, Yahweh called out to Abraham. "Take your beloved son up to the mountain in Moriah and build there an altar."

"Why, my Lord?"

"As testimony to your faith, you will sacrifice your firstborn son on a pyre."

Abraham's world lurched and his breathing stopped. For some time he was aware of nothing but the pounding in his chest. Blood throbbed in his ears. He opened his mouth to speak, but words could not express the pain he felt, as if a dagger had pierced his heart and was held fast. He said nothing.

The next morning, Abraham and two servants cut some wood and tied the sticks into two bundles, which the slaves carried on their backs. Abraham threw a saddle over the ass, hoisted Isaac, and climbed on behind the boy. The small party made their way toward Moriah.

After traveling for three days, they saw the mountain in the distance.

"Isaac and I will go on alone," Abraham told his servants.

Isaac carried the wood, and Abraham brought his knife and a clay pot bearing a small fire.

As they walked along, Isaac asked, "Father, I see the wood and the fire for an offering of a lamb, but where is the animal to be slaughtered?"

"When the time comes," Abraham responded, "God will see to it."

In a short distance, they glimpsed a coney as it darted behind a rock.

"Did you see that, Father?" Isaac asked laughing. "The coney is a funny-looking animal. Its ears are so small, and it doesn't even have a tail!"

"Yes, son," Abraham responded flatly, "it is a very strange little beast." But inside, his heart was tearing.

Once they reached the mountaintop, Abraham gathered stones and slowly piled them up to build an altar. When it was finished, Abraham said to Isaac, "Son, come rest yourself here." Isaac lay down and, being very tired from the long journey, soon fell fast asleep.

Abraham stood before the pillar on which Isaac slept, gently binding the boy's hands and feet. Before him lay the promise of a future born to his wife, Sarah, in her ninetieth year. Isaac was truly a gift from God, this much Abraham knew.

Everything that the century of Abraham's own life had become was now focused on the point of the knife that he raised high, poised above his son's breast. Tears streamed from Abraham's eyes.

"Why!" he thought as he flexed his forearms to grip the handle and point the blade down toward Isaac's heart. "What will this prove, Lord?"

His shoulders turned as he raised the blade higher.

"Yahweh, this is the same blade with which I was circumcised to honor our covenant. What you have given, would you have me take away by my own hand?"

Abraham could see that the rending of his son's heart would open a door that would lead to the rest of his life.

"But what life would that be, for a man who has murdered his one and only son?"

Then a calm came over Abraham. A resolve. He hoisted the blade to the top of its arc and stared, glassy eyed, into the distance, beyond the pain that seared his heart.

At the moment that the knife responded to his intent and began its journey home, the voice of an angel cried out.

"Abraham, wait!"

"Yes!" cried Abraham. "What would you have me do!"

"Sheath your knife. Your faith has saved Isaac, your only begotten son, whom you would have killed at Yahweh's command to prove your love."

The knife fell from Abraham's trembling hands and clattered on the stones by his feet.

"Yahweh is moved by your faith and devotion," said the angel. "Blessed be Isaac and all the generations that will be born through him."

In a tearful blur of relief and profound joy, Abraham untied the bindings from Isaac. When the boy awoke, Abraham helped him down from the altar.

At that moment Abraham saw that, nearby, the horns of a ram had become stuck in a juniper bush. He walked to the ram and thankfully drove his knife into its side. The beast kicked and fell, then its chest was still. Abraham wiped his knife. He cradled the ram in his arms and placed it on the altar. At last, Abraham lit the firewood and made a burnt offering to Yahweh.

Now the voice of the angel became the very voice of Yahweh. "My servant, Abraham, your faith has moved me to the depths, that you would sacrifice your only son as a sign of our covenant. In time, your descendants will spread out across this desert as waves break upon the shore of the sea. And they will be as many as the grains of sand and the stars in the night sky. The walls of your enemies will crumble before you, and nations will count your heirs as a multitude and a blessing."

Abraham looked up toward heaven and cried aloud, "Yahweh has appeared on this mountain."

He gently took hold of Isaac and turned the boy to face him. Then he bent down and embraced his son for a long silence.

Isaac hugged him in return. "Father," said Isaac. "It is me." And Abraham wept.

When he had dried his eyes, Abraham took Isaac's hand and led him down the mountain to where the servants were still waiting. He hoisted Isaac up onto the back of the ass, climbed again behind him, pulled on the reins, and returned to Beersheba.

## — 12 —

Years passed and the child Isaac grew into a young man. Sarah and Abraham were proud of their son, of how he was kind and respectful to every person, no matter his or her station in life.

"One day, Isaac will be a great man, the leader of a nation!" Abraham often said to Sarah when they were alone.

"Yes, husband, that may be," she replied, "but first we must find him a wife. The tree cannot bear fruit without the flower."

"Our son is not a bee!"

"More's the shame," she replied. "A little honey might help him lure someone sweet into his hive."

"Sarah, you surprise me sometimes," said Abraham, smiling.

"Do you think there is anything I have not seen or heard?" she said, reaching out and patting the back of his hand.

Sarah was now a woman of 127 years who was renowned and revered in that land. She lived with Abraham in the city of Hebron, which was called at the time Kiriath-arba.

One morning when Abraham awoke, there was a leaden silence in the tent. The familiar breathing of Sarah was absent—something that he had grown so accustomed to during their long life together that he often noticed their breaths coming in the same rhythm. He sensed that she was still present, but he heard nothing.

For a time, Abraham could not bring himself to look toward Sarah. He knew what his eyes would find. Then, slowly, he turned his head and saw that her spirit no longer dwelled within.

Abraham slid his hand over to touch the cold skin of Sarah's cheek. He mourned in silence as scenes of their full life played through his mind's eye. After all their journeys together—the flight to Egypt, the road to Hebron, sharing the birth of their only child—he was grateful for the life they had shared. But it was not the will of Yahweh for Sarah to witness the blossoming of Isaac's life. And it was this thought that finally brought tears to his eyes and pangs into his heart.

Later that day, Abraham asked the Hittites for permission to bury Sarah in the land where they lived.

The Hittites considered Abraham to be a true servant of God. "You may choose any tomb you desire," they told him.

Bowing out of respect, Abraham asked to bury Sarah in a cave owned by Ephron, the son of Zohar, at a place called Machpelah. "I will gratefully accept your offer," Abraham said, "but I would pay Ephron what the land is worth."

Ephron was present, and as all of his people watched and listened, he said, "It will be my honor to offer the land where the cave is found as a gift."

Again Abraham bowed and said, "Your kindness knows no bounds and is most welcome in this time of need. Yet, I would be glad to pay for the land."

"It is a trifle between us," said Ephron. "The land is worth four hundred shekels of silver."

"That is fair," said Abraham as he accepted the price. Then he weighed out the pieces of silver as the Hittites bore witness.

Just before nightfall, all had been made ready. Dressed in her finest clothes and wrapped in a white burial shroud, Sarah was laid in the tomb aglow with the fire of sunset. Abraham went in alone to say his last respects. He brought with him a black scarf, which he draped over Sarah's neck.

"Here, my dearest heart, my angel. Your beloved ring doves will carry you to everlasting joy in the kingdom of Yahweh. Soon, I will join you there, and we will both, at last, be at peace."

When Abraham emerged from the tomb, he motioned with the silent sweep of an arm to a group of his closest kinsmen who waited next to a large stone. On Abraham's signal, the ground shook as the stone was rolled across the opening of the cave.

Abraham turned to see the last rays of sun wash across the broad plains of Machpelah. There, in the distance, Abraham saw a large, wizened old tree. Himself. The Oak of Mamre.

# ISAAC AND REBEKAH

*And there were angels of God*
*going up it and coming down.*

Genesis 28:13

— 1 —

The blustery wind pelted Isaac with sand as he climbed into the hills near Moriah. There was a palpable sense of power in that place, of the elemental. Being there always imbued him with an excited energy, a vitality that made him glad to be alive.

After a long climb up a moderate talus slope, Isaac wended his way through some large boulders until he came to a crawl space that led out onto a ledge at the top of a steep cliff. From that high escarpment, peering through the space between two large rocks, Isaac could see the vast lands of his people—a gift from Yahweh—a rolling expanse that touched the horizon.

Isaac was careful to keep well back from the ledge. He didn't want to alarm the two eaglets that perched there, hunched in their nest of large sticks and waiting for the eagles to return with food, perhaps a quail, a coney, or even a newborn kid. With each breeze generated by the thermals that rose up the cliff face, a rank odor wafted through the cleft in the rocks, a smell that was fed by the old bones and decaying scraps of meat that littered the ledge surrounding the eagles' nest.

Every time Isaac had visited the nest prior to that day, the adult eagles had been present, tearing their prey into small enough chunks for the eaglets to eat, silently riding the thermals in the airspace near the ledge, or simply perched, staring out into the distance with eyes that, to Isaac, seemed to take pride in the broad verge of *their* territory.

But on this afternoon, the eaglets, who were now almost as large as the adults, had been left alone while their parents went off to hunt.

Taking the large skin bag off of his shoulder, Isaac untied the draw-string and opened the mouth wide. He pulled out a pair of thick hide gloves and put one of them on, then held a strong cord in his other hand, at the ready. Working quickly, he scrambled through the crevice, firmly gripped one of the napping eaglets by the beak, and, before the bird could squawk its alarm call, looped several lashings of the cord to bind its mouth. Isaac used another cord to tie the hapless chick's legs together, being careful to avoid the piercing talons. Once the eaglet was safely inside the bag, Isaac tied it snugly and carried it as he crawled back through the crevice. As quickly as he could go and still keep his footing, he scrambled down the mountainside then strode back along the trail toward home.

Abraham greeted his son as he returned from another long foray in the desert wilderness. Isaac often wandered far from his father's home. A tall, handsome man who exuded a quiet strength, he was well trained in the arts of falconry and fighting. Still, Abraham worried about him.

"What did you find today, out in the middle of nowhere?"

"Father, I climbed the cliff where the eagles are nesting. Here is one of the eaglets."

"What are you going to do with that? Eat it?"

"No, Father, I am going to train it as one would a falcon."

"Is that possible?"

"Are *you* really asking *me* if something is possible? You who have built a life on accomplishments that most men would consider impos-sibilities. 'Have faith Isaac.' Do those words have a familiar ring?"

"Sarcasm, Son? It was a simple question. You are my heir—the wealthiest unmarried man of your age in the Negeb. I just want you to be happy. So I worry about you."

Abraham stared at his son. He knew that Isaac's difficult moods were rooted in the time when he lost his mother at a young age. That history fed Isaac's naturally laconic nature. When he was not in the company of his immediate friends and family, he preferred to be alone. Isaac enjoyed hunting and often took long walks into the hinterlands.

He usually brought a sleeping roll and went out for several days on foot, especially when sadness over the loss of his mother overtook his spirit.

Hunting and hiking, though, were just excuses for Isaac to do what he loved most of all—taking trips to observe the winged creatures that inhabited his world. He was fascinated by birds of prey: the magnificent lanner falcon with its deep-set eyes and wings that seemed to slice the very air, the agile kite with its deeply forked tail, and above all else the golden eagle whose wingspan was greater even than the considerable height of Isaac's lithe frame. The few eagle feathers that Isaac had found during the spring molt were among his prized possessions.

Over the coming months, Isaac befriended the eaglet he had caught. He adapted his considerable falconry skills to training this new bird for the hunt. He grew to love the young eagle, to revel in its power and majesty. This scion of the birds that fly highest became his emblem—an apt symbol of his lineage. It possessed a regal nature, was extremely long lived, and attained heights that afforded a superior vantage point—a broad perspective and freedom to soar.

## — 2 —

With Sarah gone from his life and Isaac grown into a young man, Abraham had far too much time alone to contemplate his fate.

"I am old," he thought, "and I feel my age. Yahweh has given me many blessings, but there is one last thing I must do. I have to find a wife for Isaac. He is long past the age, but has yet to marry."

Abraham walked out of his tent and approached Eliezer, a loyal servant who had become a respected elder in that household.

"Eliezer, you have served my family and taken care of my lands for two generations. I have a request that I would only ask of you because of the bond of trust we share."

"Master, I am honored."

"Place your hand upon my groin and swear an oath to me."

Eliezer did as Abraham requested, following an ancient custom for entering into an unbreakable promise.

"Pledge in the name of Yahweh, God of all creation …"

"I do," said Eliezer, who then removed his hand.

"I want Isaac to marry a woman from my homeland in Haran, from among the families of my own relations. He will not, under any circumstance, marry a woman from the Canaanites where we live now."

"As you wish," Eliezer replied. "Do you want me to go to Haran to find him a wife?"

"Yes."

"And shall I take Isaac with me?"

"No!" cried Abraham. "This may not be the home of my kinfolk, the place of my father, but Yahweh led us here and promised that our heirs would inherit this land. Isaac will remain here. This is where he will raise his family. I am trusting you in this matter."

"I will honor that trust with my life," said Eliezer. "But I am an old man. It has been many years since I traveled the old roads that lead to Haran."

"Don't worry. An angel of God will lead your way."

"There is one last thing," said Eliezer.

"What is that?"

"Suppose I choose a wife for Isaac, but she does not want to return here to marry him?"

"Then you have fulfilled your duty to me and will be free of this obligation from that day forward."

Eliezer ordered the servants to load ten camels with samples of Abraham's finest possessions: gold jewelry set with precious stones, finely embroidered tapestries, small sculptures, spices, and incense. When all was ready, Eliezer rode the lead camel that led the caravan away from the house of Abraham, winding through the fields, beyond the grazing lands, and into the desert beyond.

After traveling for several days, Eliezer was caught in a storm that sent waves of dust and sand washing across the landscape. The long, hard wind forced Eliezer to don a kerchief to cover his head and mouth as protection from the gritty air.

When he came to a large stand of ancient juniper trees that offered a bit of shelter, Eliezer tied off the lead camel to a branch. Eliezer had grown tired fighting against the gale, so he sat upon a stone to rest and bent over with his back to the wind. The old man glanced next to him and saw an ancient, gnarled juniper that was also leaning over—bent by a century of yielding to the will of the wind. Its bark was furrowed, and the needles were nearly gone from its branches.

The shape of the aged tree so nearly mirrored Eliezer's as he sat huddled against the wind, that he said aloud, "Little tree, I am well aware of what the years have done to my body. There is no need to mock me."

When the storm abated, Eliezer continued along the roads that led to Upper Mesopotamia, to a place called Aram Naharaiim, "Aram of the rivers," in the land of Haran.

"How will I know when I have found a suitable wife for Isaac?" he wondered as he worked his way across the harsh land. Just before he reached the main well at the edge of the city, Eliezer decided. "I will go to the well at the edge of Haran with my camels, looking for water. The first young woman who offers me a ladle of water and also gives water to my camels is the one I will choose."

After he had been sitting near the well for a time, a girl in fine dress came over to him.

"You look thirsty," she said.

"Yes, I have just made a long journey," Eliezer replied.

"Give me your flask and I will fill it for you," she said.

When she returned with the water, Eliezer pulled a long drink from the flask, then said, "You are most kind." With a polite nod of her head, she walked away.

As the day wore on, Eliezer watched as many young women stared in his direction with expressions of curiosity, pity, or, occasionally, disdain.

In the late afternoon, during the heat of the day, a lovely young woman saw Eliezer.

She thought it strange to see a tired old man standing by the well, as if he was expecting someone. His camels were baking in the sun, fully loaded with belongings that must have weighed a thousand shekels.

She filled her large clay pot and walked over to greet him.

"Sir, hold out your flask and I will fill it," she said to Eliezer.

After this was done, Rebekah poured water into each of the drinking pouches that were hanging from the camels' mouths, making numerous trips back to the well to refill the jug with enough water to service all twelve camels. When she was finished, Rebekah walked back to Eliezer.

"You are the most generous soul I have met since leaving my own land many days ago," said Eliezer.

"How long have you been waiting here?" she asked.

"For about half the day and for nearly two dozen unsuitable prospects. Most of the young women who came to this well looked at me with suspicion, as if I was a dirty old man!"

"I can't imagine why," said Rebekah with the vague hint of a smile.

"What is your name?"

"Rebekah."

"Hold out your hand, Rebekah, you who have quenched my thirst and that of my camels."

Eliezer gently took Rebekah's hand and gave her a small gold ring. Eliezer pointed to her nose. Rebekah, understanding, took the ring and slipped it into a piercing in her nostrils.

"Now give me your wrists, my dear." Eliezer then put two heavy gold bracelets onto her wrists. They were etched with intricate designs of the oak and the dove, markings of the house of Abraham.

"Thank you, they are beautiful," said Rebekah. She studied the designs for a few moments, then said, "These etchings are familiar to me. We have an altar at home that is adorned with these same symbols."

Eliezer's heart leaped with joy and relief. "I would be honored to see those designs. Whose family do you come from?" asked Eliezer.

But Rebekah did not answer directly. "My father would be ashamed if I did not offer you a place in our house for the night. Our stables are also large, and we could give your camels food and rest before you continue your journey."

"Pray, go to your house and speak with your family. Tell them what has happened and that I would accept their hospitality."

When she arrived home, Rebekah shared the story, then showed them the ring and the bracelets.

Unable to contain his excitement, her brother Laban ran back to the well and invited the man to their house. When Eliezer arrived there, he met Rebekah's mother, and her father, Bethuel.

"Where did you obtain this jewelry?" asked Rebekah's mother. "These designs have been in our family for two generations."

"What family would that be?"

"My husband is Bethuel."

"I am not familiar with that name," said Eliezer, disappointed.

"Then, perhaps you know of Bethuel's parents."

"And what are *their* names?" asked Eliezer.

"They are Milcah and Nahor."

"Praise God!" cried Eliezer. "Nahor is the brother of my master, Abraham. And Rebekah, then, is his granddaughter! How mysterious are the ways of Yahweh, and how generous he is to my master."

"Come," said Bethuel. "My servants will wash your feet after such a long journey."

Laban and his servants took the burdens from the camels, laid straw in the stable, and placed fodder for their food.

"Come and eat with us at our table," Bethuel invited. "Join us for a meal."

"First, I must tell you why I have come here."

"Then at least sit and rest while you say your piece," Bethuel implored.

Eliezer sat on the edge of a chair and leaned on the table, facing toward Bethuel.

"As you know, your uncle Abraham is a wealthy man. Over the years, he has been blessed with stores of precious metals, large tracts of land, and the animals that graze in those fields. His house has many servants and slaves. But he lost his beloved Sarah some years ago. That was when the light began fading from his life. Since Sarah's passing, Abraham has not been the same person he once was. Now, when he looks at the face of his son Isaac, Abraham sees the eyes of his wife Sarah. If Abraham had to choose, I believe he would give up everything to assure the happiness of Isaac—who remains his strongest connection to Sarah."

"It is well put," said Bethuel. "But why have you—who are yourself getting on in years—why have you made this long and difficult journey with a small fortune lashed to the backs of these camels.

"Abraham asked me to come to Haran to find a wife for Isaac from among the women of his own kinfolk. I gave him my vow that I would do this one last thing for him. At times, during this journey, that vow has felt like a curse. When I arrived here, I waited by the well for a young woman who would be generous to myself and my camels, who were also in need of water. Rebekah was the only young woman who showed compassion. She brought water to me, then returned many times from the well to bring the same refreshment to each of my camels."

"And the jewelry?" queried Laban, who was also sitting and listening among them.

"I vowed that I would offer the ring and bracelets to the young woman whom I would ask to become Isaac's wife. You can only imagine my joy, and wonder, to discover that Rebekah is the granddaughter of Abraham's brother!"

Eliezer paused and slowly looked around the table. He caught and held the eye of every person seated there, in turn. The last person he looked at was Bethuel.

"Now," he continued, "I ask you, your family, and Rebekah herself whether she would return with me to the lands of Abraham and agree to become Isaac's wife."

Relaxing for the first time since he had left the house of Abraham, Eliezer leaned back in his chair, opened his arms wide, and exclaimed, "It is done! I have fulfilled my vow. However you decide, it is out of my hands. Now, what is your answer?"

There was a long pause, during which Bethuel and Laban caught each other's eyes as if speaking a silent language born of familiarity.

"Yahweh sent you to us …," said Bethuel.

"And Yahweh has presented us with this request," Laban continued.

Then they both replied enthusiastically, "Who are we to refuse such a blessing?"

"Rebekah will return with you to become Isaac's wife," Bethuel concluded.

"Praise God!" said Eliezer, who slumped back in his chair, feeling both grateful and relieved. Then, with an exaggerated air that turned everyone's joy into laughter, he stood up, took the kerchief from around his neck and used it for a dramatic flourish as he bowed to each and every member of the family.

When everyone had finished embracing, kissing, and congratulating each other, Eliezer walked quickly to the camels, untied a large cloth bag, and carried it over to the table around which they were seated. The bag was full of bundles bound with fine cloth. Eliezer pulled them from the bag and gave a particular parcel to each member of Rebekah's family. Some contained jewelry made from gold and silver and inlaid with precious gems. From others came candle holders, clothing, and other treasures.

By sunset, a small feast had been hastily prepared.

"You are so kind and generous," said Eliezer. "I have never been greeted with such open arms. And the feast: You treat me like royalty!"

"More than a king!" said Bethuel.

"What, then?" asked Eliezer.

"Family!" replied Laban.

"Blood is stronger, even, than the bonds of gold," said Bethuel.

"If that is true, Father," said one of the other children, "then perhaps you will trade me that gold amulet you are wearing around your neck for this piece of blood sausage."

"What!" cried Bethuel, as laughter rippled across the room.

"Husband," came another voice in mocking earnestness, "I think you have met your match."

There was no end to the questions that Rebekah's family posed to Eliezer. Their curiosity about the house of Abraham was insatiable. They ate, drank, and celebrated well into the night.

When the evening was winding down, Bethuel raised a cup of wine. "Blessed be Rebekah and Isaac. That their offspring may be as many as the …"

"Stars in the sky," said Laban.

"Grains of sand," added Bethuel's wife.

"Fleas on a camel," said one of the children.

"Specks of d … d … dust," stammered Eliezer, who was now both exhausted *and* moved by the spirit—of the grape.

"All right, all right, that's enough. You all know the blessing—lots of little ones!" Bethuel bellowed. "Now, to bed!"

The next morning, Eliezer went to Bethuel.

"You are the master of this house," he said. "I know that Abraham would be most pleased if Rebekah accompanies me on the journey back to his home in the Negeb."

"Please," Bethuel replied. "Everything has happened so quickly. Give her some time to prepare."

"With all respect," said Eliezer, "please grant this last request."

"Your loyalty to Abraham is to be commended," said Bethuel. "Come, let us ask Rebekah what she wishes."

"Daughter, you have been requested to return to the house of Abraham this very morning, where you will marry his son Isaac. What do you say?"

Rebekah took Bethuel's hand and said excitedly, "Father, please, I will miss you all. But I would leave this morning if it is your will."

Bethuel drew her to him and kissed the top of her head. "You have my blessing, Little Quail." Then, with a palpable sense of how the turning of life stretches the heart, he looked off to the horizon and saw the morning sun rise through a haze of tears.

## — 3 —

At that time, Isaac was off on another sojourn into the wilds. After walking for a few days, he came to the well known as Lahai Roi. Isaac sensed that there was a certain power about the place, the "well of the seeing spirit." What he did not know is that this was where Hagar had once seen an angel of God reflected in the water, a vision that had prophesied the future for her son, Ishmael.

Isaac peered over the edge and stared at his reflection. "I have seen forty years and am no longer a young man," he said to himself. "What, oh seeing spirit, do you hold for *my* future?"

Disappointed when no answer came, Isaac continued to amble out across the grassland. He was so deep in thought that he didn't notice the camels moving slowly along the trail.

From her height atop one of the camels, Rebekah saw a man in the distance. She turned to Eliezer and said, "Look, over there, someone is coming toward us. But I don't think he has seen us yet. Do you know who it is?"

"Yes, I recognize his robes and his easy gate," Eliezer replied. "That is Isaac, my dear. You are looking at the man you are going to marry."

"He cannot yet see my face!" said Rebekah, as she pulled down her veil.

One of the camels snorted and the sound caused Isaac to start from his revery. He changed course and walked in that direction.

"Eliezer," he yelled and waved when he recognized the elder servant who had been a trusted companion since his birth. When Isaac reached the group, he greeted Eliezer, then turned toward the young woman hidden under a veil.

Looking back at Eliezer, Isaac asked, "Is there someone you would like me to meet?"

"In due time," said Eliezer. "All in due time, Master Isaac."

Isaac walked alongside the caravan on its final leg of the journey from Haran. By nightfall, they had reached the house of Abraham.

One of the children was the first to see them coming. He ran to the tent of Abraham yelling, "Eliezer is coming, and a young woman is riding with him!"

Abraham soon emerged from the tent, already dressed in his finery. All the preparations for a wedding had been made in Eliezer's absence, in anticipation of his return with a bride for Isaac.

Abraham greeted Eliezer, then took the reins of the first camel and led the caravan over to a clearing in which a wedding tent had been raised. It was festooned with ribbons, and a fine rug had been rolled out, leading to the doorway. Rebekah was ushered away by a woman, and Abraham led Isaac to his own tent to help him prepare for the wedding.

Once they had entered the tent, Isaac said, "Father, why the rush? There is plenty of time for a wedding."

"How old are you, my son?"

"Forty years now."

"And not getting any younger, I see," said Abraham as he raised an eyebrow and looked Isaac over. "Here, put these clothes on. You're getting married tonight, and not another word about it!"

The ceremony was extravagant, but brief. When Isaac raised Rebekah's veil to kiss her, he caught his breath and hesitated.

"What is it?" she asked.

"I never hoped or expected that you would be so beautiful," Isaac whispered. He took both of her hands and kissed her gently. Then he held her left hand in his right, turned to face the wedding guests, raised their hands up, and said aloud, "Everyone, please welcome Rebekah, my wife, into our house!" Cheers rang out and split the silence of a desert night.

Later that evening, over dinner, the smell of wine and bread and spices scented the air. While the sweet notes from lute and lyre drifted through the crowd, Eliezer recounted for Abraham and all who sat at his table the odyssey of his journey to the well in Haran. He recalled how he had met Rebekah and the warm reception that he had received in the house of Bethuel.

When Eliezer came to the conversation during the feast, he gilded the lily. "And when Bethuel realized that I made such a treacherous journey unscathed, he observed to all who were present, 'Surely, Eliezer, Abraham must have trusted you because you are both brave and bold.'"

As he spoke these words, Eliezer glanced over toward Rebekah, but he could not discern her reaction through the veil. But as he suspected, Rebekah noticed Eliezer's embellishments and saw how the tale had already begun to grow in the telling.

When Eliezer's story had at last spun out, the night was deepening. Isaac led Rebekah quietly down to their tent. He removed her veil and kissed her softly. By the glow of a lamp whose oil had been scented with myrrh, Isaac saw in Rebekah's eyes a part of himself that he had lost many years ago with the passing of his mother. They lay quietly for a long time. While they passed their first night as husband and wife, Isaac could feel that something inside of him was being made whole. His vision began to shift away from the pain of the past and into the promise of the dawn.

# — 4 —

Hope pervaded the house of Abraham during the first months after the wedding of Isaac and Rebekah, hope for the beginning of a new generation. Hope that went unfulfilled.

Years passed, and Abraham could see the disappointment in Isaac's eyes—a reminder of his own long childless years of marriage with Sarah. Isaac ached to see his own child cradled in his father's arms. One morning, in his 175th year, Abraham did not arrive at table to break the fast.

"Where is he?" asked Isaac.

"At his age, don't you think he has earned a few more hours of rest?" Rebekah replied. "Let him sleep."

Concerned, Isaac went to his father's tent, opened the door flap, and stepped inside.

"Father?" he said anxiously.

"Yes, Son," Abraham replied. "Come closer."

As Isaac approached, he could hear that Abraham's breathing was shallow and strained. He sat down next to where his father lay.

"My time is short," said Abraham. "Listen closely. There is something I must tell you while I still can."

When Abraham had finished speaking, Isaac sensed an eerie stillness in the gray light of the tent. A chill ran through him, and he knew that the spirit of Abraham, the great oak on which his house was rooted, had gone home to Yahweh.

Isaac knelt down by Abraham's body and put his hand over that of his father.

"All these years you have provided for us and protected this house, like the branches of a great tree." said Isaac. "I will miss you, Father. Now it is up to me to carry on your covenant with Yahweh. God willing."

Arrangements were made for Abraham's burial. Although Isaac did not look forward to an encounter with Ishmael, a message was sent telling him of his father's death and of the place and time of the burial. Ishmael was Isaac's half brother, whom Abraham had fathered with Hagar, a slave woman from Egypt who once served Isaac's mother, Sarah.

After the memorial ceremony, a smaller group of close family accompanied the patriarch's body to the place of burial in the cave of Machpelah, overlooking the plains of Mamre.

When they arrived at the tomb, Ishmael was waiting there with some members of his own family.

Isaac walked over to greet him. "Brother," he said as he embraced Ishmael, "this is a sad day."

"Thank you for sending a messenger to me so swiftly," said Ishmael.

"You are my family, also," Isaac replied. "It was only right that you should know."

The body of Abraham was laid carefully in the tomb, next to the body of his wife, Sarah, whom Abraham had buried there twenty-eight lonely years before.

Then, members of the family took turns going into the tomb to say goodbye and to pay their respects.

Isaac went in last. He had woven a wreath of sprigs from the branches of the Oak of Mamre. He placed the wreath on Abraham's head and kissed his hand one last time. Isaac came out of the tomb and watched as it was sealed with the stone. He then walked past everyone in attendance and out alone into the desert night.

Engulfed in grief and uncertainty, Isaac wandered, with no idea where his feet were taking him. The cool, pungent desert air rustled his robes. An owl voiced its mournful call in the distance. Isaac looked in that direction, grateful for the light of a nearly full moon to help him avoid the dangers of stepping on a poisonous adder or of being bitten by a scorpion. When Isaac finally stopped to rest, he was standing by the Well of Lahai Roi. Instinctively, he fell to his knees. He could hold back the tears no more.

"Hear me, Isaac, son of Abraham," said Yahweh.

"What would you have me do, my God?"

"Here, in the land of your father, I will make you the scion of a great tree that will bear the fruit of multitudes. And your name shall be a blessing upon the tongues of the faithful."

# — 5 —

Ishmael and his family also left the tomb immediately after the burial. He felt a warmth toward Isaac that he had seen returned in his brother's eyes. Growing up together they had come to be best friends. Those feelings still lay buried somewhere beneath the hard layers that had accrued over the ensuing years.

Although Isaac was still without child, Ishmael had married young and already had several children. His first son, Nebaioth, was himself a father. In time, Ishmael's wife would bear twelve sons, including his last, Kedemah.

Even though Ishmael felt compassion toward his brother, because Isaac's wife had been unable to bear a child, he was also torn with feelings of resentment. He still harbored ill-will toward Isaac, who had inherited Abraham's land and possessions—half of which Ishmael believed rightfully belonged to him. But for the sake of their father's memory, he kept all this inside when he saw Isaac and did not speak about it to anyone.

For his entire life, Ishmael had been rebellious—a reaction against the way he and his mother, Hagar, had been treated by Isaac's mother, Sarah. His feelings were further enflamed by the knowledge that Abraham had acquiesced to Sarah's wishes. Ishmael had taken advantage of every opportunity over the years to engage Isaac in argument and strife.

Ishmael was a formidable foe who was at home in the wilderness—as wild and untamable as the bears of Mount Lebanon. He was renowned as the most skilled practitioner of the art of falconry throughout the land. Ishmael seemed to have an intuitive connection with his finest and most favorite falcon, whom he had named Anakim. Just one look from its master, or the slightest throat sound, and the bird knew exactly what Ishmael was communicating. Denizens of those parts wondered how Ishmael could possibly know where people were at all times, both friends and foes. They would be out walking close to home, or traveling on a long journey, or shepherding up in the hills, and Ishmael would appear to greet them, or fight them, as he wished. It was as if he followed others in his dreams and knew exactly where to find them with no foreknowledge. Some said that he found this sight through the eyes of his Anakim. Others went so far as to say that the two were as one.

A viper is its true self when it poisons its prey. A wasp's sting is meant to be used. Like these creatures, our darkest feelings lie in wait until the moment comes to act on them.

It took nothing more than a minor argument between a handful of relatives at the well of Lahai Roi to stir the simmering conflict between Isaac and Ishmael. To each house, the well evoked strong emotions because it represented an important source of water as well as a family history and spiritual connection to Yahweh. Isaac, who did not want to fight his brother, argued for sharing the well, but Ishmael taunted and insulted him, then insisted on a fight to settle the dispute.

"What would you have us do—kill each other?" asked Isaac. "Would that satisfy your vengeance?"

"Of course, Brother, you would dismiss my claims, for half of what you own is rightfully mine."

"I will not fight you. Neither would I risk leaving my wife and the members of my house without me. Nor would I want it on my conscience that I killed my own brother and deprived his family of a provider and protector."

"I have a proposal," said Ishmael.

"Speak."

"Let us both offer something of the scent of our two birds to the other: my falcon to your eagle, and your eagle to my falcon."

"What! You would have us settle our dispute in the skies?"

"Yes, Brother, or is even *that* combat too much for your weak stomach?"

"And to the victor?" asked Isaac.

"The well of Lahai Roi."

So it was agreed. But Isaac's heart was torn. He remembered their childhood together in the days before Sarah had forced Hagar and Ishmael to leave their home and wander in the desert. In those early years, Isaac had been close to his older brother. Some had said they were inseparable. Isaac had always held out hope that one day, when the conflicts and complexities of their parents' relationships had begun to fade into the past, he and his brother would mature and reconcile. But now he saw that such a wish was folly and would never come to pass.

On the appointed day, hundreds of their kinfolk gathered out on the plains to the west of the well of Lahai Roi. Isaac brought his eagle, and Ishmael, his falcon. Each gave the other a cloth that held the strong scent of the other's bird. The birds were given commands to hunt. Then, on signal, Isaac and Ishmael released the birds' jesses and watched them rise into the sky.

The eagle flapped slowly upward, caught a thermal, and rode it well, circling higher and higher until it appeared small against the pastel blue of midday. Ishmael's falcon, which had already surmounted the height attained by the rising eagle, began to maneuver in smaller and smaller circles, sizing up its prey. Then it started to swipe at the eagle in rapid stoops, searching for a weakness, a vulnerable place to attack. This happened so high up that those watching from below could see very little.

Time and again, the falcon's fierce attacks drove home, inflicting deep wounds: cuts on the nape of the eagle's neck, broken tail feathers, deep gouges along its back. As it seeped blood, the eagle began to weaken and soar lower in the sky. The crowd could now see how the aerial drama was unfolding.

"Look," someone said, pointing to the eagle. "The falcon is too swift and agile for such a large, slow-moving bird. The contest is not a fair match."

"Yes," said Ishmael. "The eagle is like its master's house: too large and encumbered to fight, even in self-defense."

At last the falcon decided to finish off its wounded, weakening foe. It flew higher and higher toward the sun, as it often does to confuse its prey by blinding any gaze that tries to follow. At the apex of its flight, the falcon folded its wings and fell, accelerating to a streak of feather, beak, and talon. As it reached the eagle, it opened its wings to break its fall, violently switched its tail fan, rolled upside down, and came up under the eagle, with talons poised to tear at the great bird's vulnerable belly.

But just as the falcon made its fateful turn and was concentrating on intricate movements of muscle and feather to accomplish the bold maneuver, the eagle saw one brief opening. In a quick jab of deadly force, the eagle's powerful beak shot out and locked down onto the throat of the falcon, instantly snapping its neck. Shrieks rose up from the crowd.

For an instant, the eagle held onto the falcon, which now hung limp and twitching in its beak. Then it opened its massive jaws and released the lifeless bird. With one wing askew, the falcon spiraled down, down, down, as a winged seed falls from a cedar of Lebanon. Breathless, the crowd watched as the falcon landed in a limp heap that raised a small, silent cloud of the dusty red desert earth, too far away to make a sound that their ears could hear.

Ishmael said nothing. He walked alone into the distance, bent over to pick up his faithful bird, and wept. No one in the crowd spoke. They stood for a time, torn between their loyalties to Isaac and Ishmael, yet despairing over the tragedy they had just witnessed. Everyone quietly dispersed.

Although Ishmael would go on to live for 137 years in the vast desert lands that lay south of the Negeb, between the place of his birth and Assyria, the wound he brought upon himself and his beloved Anakim on that fateful day would never heal.

# — 6 —

Soon after this took place, and as if it were an omen borne of the ill will between Abraham's heirs, the rains failed and famine again spread across the land. The famine was as devastating to the people of that region as the one that Abraham and Sarah had survived by fleeing to Egypt when they were young.

Isaac walked up into the mountains to pray for guidance.

"Remain in Gerar with your people," Yahweh commanded. "You are not to go to Egypt as your father did. Listen to me, Isaac. I offer these gifts to you now because Abraham kept his faith and remembered to follow my laws and commandments. As I promised your father, I will one day give you and your heirs all the land where you now live. Your people will number as the stars. This is my blessing to you. One day, all the peoples on earth will call your name in hope that their prayers will be answered."

With crops drying up and food becoming scarce, Isaac went to Abimelech, the King of Gerar—leader of the Philistines—and asked for his help.

"Welcome," said Abimelech to Isaac, "and who is this stunning creature who accompanies you?" Abimelech kissed Rebekah's hand and bowed to her.

Isaac could see that Abimelech lusted after his wife, and he was afraid that the king might kill him to have her. So he said, "She is my sister."

"I see," said Abimelech.

And Abimelech did see. He knew that Isaac was Abraham's son and had not forgotten Abraham's deception of some years ago

"Go and keep watch on Isaac and Rebekah," Abimelech said to his most trusted servants, "but don't let them see you. If anything seems to be amiss, report back to me."

Over the years, Isaac and Rebekah had fallen very much in love. While they were in the house of Abimelech, it took all of Isaac's willpower to act chaste toward his wife and pretend that she was his sister. One day, they went for a walk in the beautiful gardens outside Abimelech's palace, where there was a small pond and a fountain.

As Isaac and Rebekah were walking by the fountain, he gave her a playful shove toward the water, and then, just as she was off balance and about to topple into the pool, Isaac pulled her back. "I have saved you, *Sister*," he said smiling.

"You almost drowned me, *Brother*," responded Rebekah wryly. "We don't have to pretend here, in this quiet garden," she whispered. "No one is watching."

Rebekah faced the fountain as Isaac stood behind and drew her close. "Some day, my love, we will have a child of our own."

At that moment, Abimelech was walking down a hallway that skirted the garden. Some movement of clothes, a flash of color by the fountain, caught his eye. When he looked down and saw Rebekah being held by Isaac, he was enraged.

"Sister, indeed!" Abimelech said darkly. "The fruit of the date does not fall far from the tree!"

"Servant!" bellowed the king, his voice echoing down the long corridor.

One of Abimelech's most trusted slaves came running. "Sire."

"Go tell Isaac that I want to see him at once!"

Isaac soon appeared before Abimelech and asked, "Why have you called me?"

"I think you know precisely why I have called you. Once again, your family has deceived me. I saw you out in the garden. Is that how you behave with your sister?"

"No," is all that Isaac said.

"Then why have you lied to me?"

"I saw how you were looking at my wife. I feared that you would take Rebekah and kill me to have her as your own."

"And what if I, or one of my other subjects, *had* slept with her. Yahweh would have brought a curse down on this house. Didn't you consider that possibility?"

Isaac bowed his head and said nothing.

"This is what I am going to do," said the king. "You and your people may till the land west of my city, but do not enter these gates again. Now go!

"And you," said Abimelech to his servant. "Tell everyone that this is my decree: Any man who touches Isaac's wife Rebekah will be killed."

That night, when Abimelech was alone with his own wife, she asked him, "Why, after all of the misery that the house of Abraham has brought to our people—and after the deception of Isaac himself— why did you give Isaac some of our best land to till?"

"It was not my desire to do so. But I remember how all our women were made barren because of the temptation Abraham brought upon me, even though I resisted it, and how every woman was made whole again because Abraham asked it of Yahweh."

"How could that have happened?" asked Abimelech's wife.

"People in the house of Abraham are Yahweh's chosen ones. Despite their dishonesties, I offer my generosity to the head of each household whenever they are in need of help. This way I hope that Yahweh will continue to bring favor to our own people."

"You are wise, husband."

"No, my dear wife. I am practical."

Some years passed. One day, Abimelech said to his wife, "The house of Abraham must truly be blessed. His son, Isaac, has come here from afar and in a short time has grown extremely wealthy. What concerns me is that this wealth has made him a powerful man in our midst. I have to find some way to put distance between us."

Abimelech went to Isaac and said, "You and your family have done well here, have you not?"

"Yes," replied Isaac. "You have been most generous and we are grateful."

"I can see that the number of people in your house is growing. There is a place where you could provide for everyone, and then some," Abimelech said. "Down in the valley of Gerar is some of the best land in our kingdom. You are welcome to take your people there, to use that land for grazing your flocks and herds and for growing your crops."

"You are truly a generous man," Isaac replied. "May Yahweh bless your house and everyone in it."

Abimelech nodded his head in consent, even as he was thinking to himself, "This fool is like the hoopoe—all show and little substance. It is fortunate that Yahweh protects his people, or they would all be scavenging for food like jackals."

Word spread and many people in those parts eventually heard about how Isaac had deceived Abimelech. Yet they watched as Isaac's people prospered. Many of Abimelech's subjects nurtured their resentments and plotted against Isaac's house. They went down to the valley of Gerar and, working by night, used sand to fill the wells that Abraham and his people had dug long ago, wells that Isaac and his kinfolk would now need for their survival.

Isaac gathered Rebekah and all of his people together to tell them of the move to the valley of Gerar.

"It is a rich land where my mother and father, Sarah and Abraham, lived many years ago. They dug some wells there that will provide all the water we will need. I am looking forward to finding one well in particular. It was dug between some rocks in a hidden grotto in the midst of a large oasis. My father described it to me many times and told me of how he and Sarah planted many beautiful flowers and trees there: scarlet lilies and sweet pomegranate, box, date, and hyssop—which they loved for the rich aroma of its leaves."

When Isaac's family reached the valley of Gerar, the first well that they discovered was filled in. They were confronted by shepherds from Abimelech's house who had been grazing their own sheep in that land for a generation.

"This is our land, and that is our water. Leave at once!" the shepherds demanded.

"No longer," Isaac replied, "Abimelech offered this land as a home for my people, as a place for us to graze our animals and grow our food."

A scuffle broke out. In the melee, a shepherd drew his dagger and deeply cut the hand of one of Isaac's servants.

"Enough," commanded Isaac, whose people greatly outnumbered the shepherds.

After the shepherds dispersed, Isaac's men dug open the well, and he named it Esek, "quarrel."

The families of Isaac's house moved deeper into the valley of Gerar. They discovered another well that had been filled in and another group of shepherds waiting for them. Again Isaac said, "Abimelech has given this land for my people to use."

"You are nothing but thieves and interlopers here!" cried the shepherds.

That well, too, was opened up, and Isaac named it, Sitnah, "accusation."

After Isaac's people moved into that land and had gained begrudging acceptance, a large new well was dug in the center of a wide open place where many of his kinfolk could obtain the water they needed.

When the new well was being blessed, Isaac said, "This new well is the heart of the valley where we can grow our food, graze our animals, and raise our families. We will call this well Rehoboth; it symbolizes that we have the space and the room to grow."

One day soon after that time, Isaac made a pilgrimage up to Beersheba to pray. Yahweh came to him, but Isaac drew back in fear.

"Do you not know me, Isaac? Surely you remember what your father, Abraham, told you about me. Abraham was loyal and steadfast. Because of his lasting faith, you will become the root of a great lineage."

Isaac knelt quietly for a long time. Before returning to his family, he erected an altar there and prayed. Later, he brought his servants back to that place and told them to dig another well in honor of Yahweh.

# — 7 —

In many ways, Isaac was now happy. His love for Rebekah and the joys they shared lifted Isaac's grief and brightened his spirits. They spent many hours trekking in the wild places where Isaac had once wandered alone, where the languid calls of owls and the wails of fox jackals had been his companions. Visiting those places caused Isaac to become aware of how he had changed. Those trips together inspired them to reflect upon what they wanted to accomplish with the rest of their lives.

Up to that time, their marriage had been one of devout love, of taking deep simple pleasure in each other's company. Yet they had been married and childless for nearly twenty years. No matter how happy they were together, there was a hole in their hearts that only the love of a child could fill.

One day, Isaac said to Rebekah, "Come with me. You and I are going alone to search for the well at the oasis."

"What is that?" she asked.

"It is a secret place that my father often spoke of. He said that when the time came I would be compelled to go there. It occupies my thoughts constantly these days. I don't think I will rest until I find that place."

"I am with you," said Rebekah, excitedly. "Let's be on our way and waste no more time."

All morning they walked, climbing a number of small hills to gain vantage points from which to discover the oasis. But the plains of Gerar spread out into a broad valley of many smaller niches that were, themselves, wide and empty. At last, in the waning hours of the day, they climbed a hill, and Rebekah exclaimed, "Look, Isaac, the setting sun is reflecting off something in the distance! And I think I see some green."

"Here," said Isaac as he held out a skin flask of water to Rebekah, "let us drink deeply and make this last push in the cool of the evening."

With renewed energy, they set out across an arid plain. There was little growing in the dry soil that yielded to their feet, which left deep impressions and raised a fine dust that caught in their eyes. Something was moving on the ground up ahead. As they approached, a flock of vultures flushed from the picked-over bones of a dead ass, which must have wandered off from someone's pasture and brayed its last call for help from the merciless desert. Rebekah and Isaac shielded their noses from the pungent smell of rotted flesh and waved off the horde of buzzing flies.

At last, they arrived at the boulders that surrounded the oasis that they had seen from afar. In the waning light of day, they searched the spaces between rocks, then crawled through a maze of small, cavelike passages toward the source of a cool, damp breeze that emanated from within.

"Isaac," cried Rebekah. "Come here. I have found it!"

Isaac crept toward the muffled sound of her voice, crawled through a low passage among the rocks, then stood, looked around, and gasped. Hidden by a tightly knit circle of boulders, and with only that one small passage to enter, was a placid pool ringed with rocks that were carefully placed.

"It is a world unto itself," said Isaac. "It is just as Abraham described it. And all these years I wondered if it was just another one of his stories. I can feel my father's presence here."

"What did he tell you about this place?" asked Rebekah.

"He said that he and Sarah would sometimes leave the families and sneak off together when they wanted to be alone. He often said that, with all of the family and servants around, it was difficult to find quiet, even in such a wide-open desolate land."

"But how can you be sure that this is *the* place he described."

Isaac took Rebekah's hand and led her over to the well. "See how these rocks are arranged in a circle around this pool? That is the secret well they dug, just the two of them. My parents came here to visit many times."

"But how could they remain here, undisturbed?"

He sat by the well, helped her down, and put his arm around her. She rested her head on his shoulder.

"This place is too far from the city and even too distant from the grazing lands for anyone to happen across it. And we didn't just find it by chance. My father used to tell me a story in which a series of hills appeared—each one with a certain shape. From each of those hills, another hill could be seen with a particular form. If he hadn't woven it into that story, I could never have remembered the way here."

"You mean that you knew exactly where we were going, all day?"

"Yes."

"Why didn't you tell me?"

"In truth, I didn't know whether he had simply told me another one of his tales, or if the story of this place was really true. I didn't want to get your hopes up, only to have both of us be disappointed if there was nothing to find."

"It is so beautiful here," said Rebekah, lifting her head to look around. "Look, there is still one patch of the lilies you said they planted here. And there is some hyssop over by the well."

She reached out a hand, picked one of the leaves, crushed, and sniffed it, then held it out for Isaac to smell.

"What do you think that old dead tree was once?" she asked.

"It may have been one of the old box trees that my father was so fond of growing, or perhaps a pomegranate. Those flowers were grown from seeds that Sarah brought here and planted. Lilies were her favorite. She often planted them where there was enough water for them to grow."

Isaac stood, then reached down to take Rebekah's hand and help her to her feet.

"What are you doing?" she asked.

"We are going to look for something."

"What? Isn't this what we came here to find?" she said gesturing around the verge of their little world.

"There is a crevice in a rock somewhere near this well. It is long and narrow and shaped like a dagger."

"What are you saying?"

"Help me find it, my love, and you shall see! If the stories that Abraham told me about this place are true, we shall discover something."

They both began to poke around the boulders that nature had piled haphazardly around the well. Much time passed. They searched in silence as the sun began to set. It was quickly becoming dark and cold.

"I don't see anything like a crevice," said Rebekah.

"Keep looking," he replied. "We're close. I know we are."

"Did Abraham tell you *where* to search?"

"The only thing Father ever said was 'Look to Yahweh.'"

Isaac stood and turned slowly in place, running the words over and over in his mind. "Look to Yahweh. Look to Yahweh."

Then he followed his instincts and searched up high. His gaze fixed on a jumble of boulders.

"Yahweh be praised!" said Isaac.

"What do you see?"

"Father told me that Yahweh spoke to him here. And he said that if I ever found this place, Yahweh would also tell me where he had hidden the very sign of his covenant. Come. Bring your head close to mine and look there," said Isaac.

Rebekah walked over to Isaac, turned, and looked up to where he was pointing.

"What?" she asked, staring toward a jumble of boulders.

"Look beyond each stone," said Isaac. "Father told me that this image is a symbol; that only when we give up our individual desires and pour forth our love and join to form a community of the faithful will we see and hear the voice of Yahweh."

Rebekah opened her heart to the words of Abraham and let her eyes take in a wider view of the rocks, straining to see something greater than the many pieces. Gradually, the image that Isaac could see also came into focus for Rebekah.

"Oh, Isaac!" she said whispering into his ear, as if to keep the secret that had remained dormant for two long generations. "I see it."

"There, my love," said Isaac, pointing upward. "That is the Mouth of God."

"Of course!" said Rebekah. "And Yahweh is smiling upon us."

Across the space from where they gazed, nearly at the top of an outcropping and silhouetted against a desert evening that glowed with the last crimson of a pomegranate sky, a pile of rocks revealed itself to be an enormous stone mouth. Although formed from boulders of great dimension and weight, the lips appeared supple and alive. It was clear that they were inviting Isaac and Rebekah—beckoning them.

"I think it is speaking to us," said Rebekah. It is saying, 'Come forward. Touch, hear, and believe.'"

"Knowing my father," said Isaac, "those stone lips are also laughing at me. They're saying, 'Son, I knew you would come, eventually, but you always did everything in your own good time. What took you so long?'"

Hands clasped tightly with anticipation, wonder, and a touch of fear, Isaac and Rebekah climbed slowly up toward the enormous mouth. When they reached it, they knelt on a large flat slab that could have been its chin and reverently ran their hands over the warm rocky lips. From inside the opening came an earthy smell.

"This is the place," said Isaac. "This is where he hid the sign of the covenant."

With those words, Isaac put his hand into the coolness of the narrow crack that marked the center of the mouth. His fingers probed deeper until it appeared to Rebekah, kneeling beside him, that his arm had been swallowed up to the shoulder. It truly looked like Isaac was being consumed.

Isaac continued to feel around inside the mouth. Then he stopped moving and his eyes shifted from side to side as he tried to picture the shape of what he was holding. Rebekah could see the muscles flex in his shoulder.

"What is it? Did you find something?" she asked impatiently.

Slowly, with great care, as if pulling a baby from a womb, Isaac maneuvered his hand through the winding turns inside the mouth as he drew back his arm. When his hand emerged, it was holding a long, thin camel-skin pouch that was bound at the top with a cord of sinew.

As if on command, Isaac and Rebekah sank down and gazed, wide-eyed, at the package.

"Isaac," Rebekah said with bated breath, "open it."

The sinew binding of the pouch disintegrated as soon as Isaac pulled at it. But the camel skin was sturdy. Isaac's hands shook as he reached inside and felt something that was smooth and contoured. He grasped the handle and slowly drew it forth. When Isaac saw what he was holding, he held it out to show Rebekah, unfolding his hand so that she could see the carving in the handle. When he opened his mouth to speak, his breath was so constricted by emotion that he could not.

Rebekah looked in wonder at the knife that Isaac held in his hand. The ivory scabbard was carved in relief to form the elegant, elongated shape of a ring dove in flight with wings folded back. As Isaac withdrew the blade, they saw that it was etched with an intricate design that evoked the twisted branches of an ancient tree. The hilt was formed of two golden oak leaves.

"It is the most beautiful thing I have ever seen," Rebekah exclaimed.

"Look at the handle!" said Isaac.

"A ram's horn?"

"Yes, love. A ram's horn. It was the last thing added to the knife."

"What does it mean?"

Isaac paused. Again his words caught in his throat. Then he spoke slowly, placing weight upon each word. "This is the Knife of the Covenant. It appeared in many of the stories that my father told. At first, it was a simple blade by which Abraham circumcised his people and consummated the bond between Yahweh and his kinfolk. When I was eight days old, Abraham circumcised me with this knife. The oak leaves are a symbol of the great sentinel Oak of Mamre, where Yahweh appeared to my father."

"And the ram's horn?"

With that question, Isaac could hold the flood no longer. Tears streamed down his face.

"That is the symbol of my father's unbounded faith in Yahweh. It is the very horn of the ram that was sacrificed in my place, on the mountain Moriah. It is a story that Abraham could only bring himself to tell me with his dying words, for he had feared all his life that if he were to tell me while he still lived, I would have questioned the depth of his love for me."

"And the ring dove?"

"That is a symbol of the enfolding love of Sarah—the love of my father's life. Each of these elements was used to embellish a simple blade. They were added over the course of his life to mark the seminal points of his own story, of the life of Sarah, and of their journey of faith and marriage together. The ring dove scabbard was the last adornment to be added—carved from a single, flawless piece of ivory."

"And you knew of this knife all along?" asked Rebekah.

"To me, this knife was mythical. My father spoke of it as if it were a living thing that carried the story of his life, of his journey to faith in Yahweh, and that held the secret of his love for Sarah. He told me that if I learned to follow my heart, to hear the call of God and to see with eyes of faith, I would one day discover the Knife of the Covenant. But it wasn't until tonight, until just now, that I realized Abraham meant it was real."

On into the night, as Rebekah listened, entranced, Isaac for the first time revealed the story of his father's sojourn of faith. Rebekah was rapt as Abraham's story lived once again beneath the desert stars. As the moon made its journey across the sky and the story unfolded, Rebekah sat cross-legged, held Isaac's hands, and looked into his eyes. At times she became agitated and squeezed his hands tightly.

Sometimes when Isaac looked, she was smiling, or tears were streaming down her face. When he came to tell the story of Moriah and the test of Abraham's faith, Rebekah became enraged and paced to quell her anger.

When, at last, Isaac fell silent, he looked up at Rebekah and saw in her eyes an intense, all-consuming love. He took her hands and returned her love with his own gaze. Then he looked upward and said, "Yahweh, we know that you have brought us here for a reason. Our faith is strong. We commit ourselves to the covenant you made with my father Abraham, and we pray that you will bless us with children of our own."

Without saying a word, Rebekah leaned over, took Isaac's face in her hands, and kissed him. Rebekah closed her eyes and pictured a young boy lying on a stone altar. She saw the hand of Abraham slowly raising a knife, higher and higher, until it was poised to strike, hovering over the heart of the man she now loved. Then she saw the knife falling and heard its blade clatter on the cold stones of a desert night, a sound that would echo down through the generations that were spared by the faithful servant of a compassionate God. They kissed each other's tears as the streams of their lives joined to form a river coursing over the desert sands.

## — 8 —

One evening not long after their visit to the oasis, Rebekah took Isaac's hand in hers. She looked up to a rising full moon and asked, "Husband, do you recall how large the moon was that rose the night we slept by the Mouth of God at the oasis."

"It was just as it is tonight," replied Isaac as he looked to the sky.

"Yes, and my womb will soon be as full."

Isaac kept staring at the moon. He squeezed Rebekah's hand tightly, drew her in close, and held her from behind. He rested his face in her hair and smelled the familiar scent that he loved—rose of Sharon.

"Faith, my love. Yahweh witnessed our love that night and has answered our prayers."

Isaac's beloved was not to have another pleasant evening for many months. Rebekah experienced sickness and cramps during her pregnancy, which went beyond anything the nursemaids had foreseen. As she neared term, her days were so difficult, her body felt so torn and wracked, that she would occasionally yell half-hearted demands like, "Just take me out into the desert and leave me to the wolves! At least that way I would be done with it!"

At wit's end, and in great discomfort, Rebekah went out to the well of Lahai Roi, near where she had first met Isaac.

"Please merciful Yahweh, help me to endure this pain. Show me what to do. My body is at war with itself."

"The strife you feel within is but a presage of what is to come after your children are born," said Yahweh.

"Children?" Rebekah asked.

"You will give birth to two boys."

Rebekah was so amazed that, again, she could only mouth a single word. "Twins?"

"Even before they are born," said Yahweh, "throughout their years as children and long after they grow up to become men, the twins will vie for power, prestige, and land. Your secondborn will come to rule over the firstborn."

A day later, Rebekah went into labor. Knowing full well the ordeal she faced, she said to her midwives, "Take me to a quiet place where my wails and screams will not be heard. And dear ladies, do prepare yourselves!"

Her labor was a seemingly endless series of painful waves—intervals of knifelike stabs during contractions were followed by quieter moments of mere agony. At last the first child began to appear.

"Look at that hair!" said the midwife. "It is as bright as the sun and as thick as a lion's mane! And the second one is right behind, holding onto his brother's heel."

When the midwife held the first baby boy up for his mother to see, Rebekah said, "We will call him Esau, 'red.'"

Mercifully, the second child emerged without delay or further complications.

Rebekah saw that he was smaller and immediately wanted to hold and shelter him. "His name will be Jacob, 'may Yahweh protect.'"

Isaac was summoned into the birthing chamber wearing the broadest smile Rebekah had ever seen. He kissed her gently and stroked her head. The midwives then placed one child in each of his arms. He cradled them there and looked at Rebekah.

"You have been so strong to endure everything that it took to bring these two into the world."

"They are lovely," said Rebekah. "I love seeing you holding our sons. But Isaac, seeing newborns in your arms does remind me that you're not a young man anymore."

"What?" he replied, "I'm only sixty years old! My father was one hundred when I was born."

"That may be so, Isaac, but in most households our boys would be grandsons."

The birth of Esau and Jacob was prescient. Esau was his father's son. He, too, grew to love the outdoors. Esau eagerly learned everything that Isaac had to teach him about tracking and reading animal signs in the wilderness. In time, Esau became a hunter whose skills were renowned and respected.

Jacob was the moon to Esau's sun. He was a gentle soul who loved to spend his time close to home. Rebekah's favorite, he watched and learned how to prepare the family meals. When Isaac and Esau returned from the hunt with a coney, a quail, or even a roebuck, Jacob would dress and clean the animals. He had a delicious way of preparing each dish—a particularly keen sense for which aromatic spices to use with every kind of meat. He could often be seen tending their herb garden, walking amid the patches of dark-scented anise, exotic cumin, and the delicate, pungent leaves of coriander. His dishes were often garnished with the flowers of saffron.

Esau once went on a long hunt and came home after many days, tired, hungry, and empty-handed. Jacob had made a spicy soup of red lentils. It smelled delicious, especially to one who had not eaten in days.

Exhausted, Esau asked, "Please, Brother, I am tired and hungry. Give me something to eat."

"What, no game to roast in the fire? No catch from the great hunter?"

"No, the game is scarce. I think that hard times have come to the wild animals. And that usually means that the same will soon happen to us."

"But surely if there is a single animal to kill for meat, you, the great hunter, could find it?"

"Stop mocking me and give me some of that soup and some bread."

"Is it that bad, then?" asked Jacob.

"Yes, I am starving!"

"All right, then. Promise me your inheritance, and I will give you something to eat."

"You're joking."

"I am serious, Brother. That's what you have to do if you want a meal."

"What! Oh, sure. A bowl of soup for my birthright? That's a fair barter in your eyes? Would that make you happy, Brother?"

Jacob looked at Esau and continued stirring the soup. "Swear it to me."

Half in jest, Esau replied, "Why not, then. What do I care about such things, right? All I need is a bedroll under the stars, my bow and arrow, and a good woman."

"Fine, then it is done," exclaimed Jacob.

"Now live up to your end of the bargain and give me something to eat. A lentil for a fortune."

Jacob held out a bowl of soup and offered a piece of hearty bread.

Esau ate his soup and bread in silence. Then he got up, shot a glance of pity at Jacob, and left.

— 9 —

Esau and Jacob had grown up, and time was mounting like dunes in the arid plains. Isaac, Rebekah, and their people had labored long and hard to plant and till the rich land that Abimelech had given to them many years before. With backbreaking work and using water from the wells that his father's people had dug, their efforts produced abundant harvests of wheat, millet, rye, and barley. Year after year, the soil yielded heavily. They built up large herds of camels and magnificent flocks of sheep that flowed like milk over the tops of the surrounding hills. Isaac and his family became extremely wealthy.

Meanwhile, back in the city of Gerar, Abimelech saw how Isaac's people had prospered once again.

"The house of Isaac is truly blessed by God," he told his wife one night after their evening meal.

"What are you worried about?"

"I'm afraid that I may have been too hasty when I ushered them out of the city."

"How could that be? You gave them some of your best land to live on."

"Yes, yes, I realize that," said Abimelech, "but some years ago our people were punished by Yahweh just because Isaac's father, Abraham, tempted me with his wife. That happened even though I resisted and did nothing wrong. What concerns me, and keeps eating at the back of my mind, is that the punishments of Yahweh are fierce, and

Yahweh's judgements against people who are not of the house of Abraham can be, well …"

"Careful, my husband!" she said.

"… Unpredictable," he concluded, although other, more severe words were coursing through his mind. "I hope that I have not angered Yahweh again," he added anxiously.

"If there is something you can do to put your mind at ease," she continued, "then, perhaps, you should do it. How much time and energy do you want to waste worrying about Isaac when you have a kingdom to look after?"

Abimelech listened. He took his counsel, Ahuzzath, and the chief of his army, Phicol, and went to meet with Isaac

When Isaac heard of their arrival, he welcomed them into his tent.

"To what do I owe this honor?" asked Isaac as he gestured for them to be seated. "Abimelech, my generous neighbor, I must inquire: Why have you come with one who you trust to keep you well advised and one who you rely on for, shall I say, protection?"

"I will be honest with you, Isaac. You, I do not fear. It is how my people are judged by Yahweh that concerns me deeply."

"Do you think that I have any control over *that*?" Isaac replied, laughing.

"Of course … no," answered Abimelech. "I would simply offer my hand in friendship—a pledge that we would each agree to live amicably as neighbors and would promise to bring no harm to each other or to our people."

"Abimelech, have no fear. You have always been kind and generous to me and to my father before me. Now come—you and your companions—join us in a meal."

Isaac and Rebekah had their servants lay out a generous repast for their guests. Well into the meal, as the food and wine flowed freely, Isaac stood and offered a blessing. Once all the guests were standing, Isaac faced Abimelech and said, "May Yahweh bless you, Abimelech, your family and all the people of your house. I offer my hand in peace."

Raising his own cup, Abimelech requited the oath. "You are truly a man of God. A blessing upon your household. I, too, offer my hand in peace."

Abimelech and Isaac reached out and shook hands to seal their word. This promise between their houses was never broken.

## — 10 —

Jacob and Esau were now grown men of forty years. Always independent and more than a step ahead of his brother, Esau was the first of Isaac and Rebekah's twins to marry. The wives he chose, Judith and Basemach, were daughters of Hittites. Because they were not from among the women of Abraham's kinsmen in Haran, Isaac and Rebekah did not approve of the marriages. In Rebekah's eyes, this was one more reason to shower her favors upon Jacob.

But Isaac was an old man who had lived for one hundred years. Darkening for a long time, his eyesight had at last failed him. Fearing that his remaining years were few, Isaac called his firstborn son to his bedside.

"Son," said Isaac as he reached out his hand, "where are you?"

"Right here, Father," Esau replied, taking Isaac's hand in his own. Isaac ran his hand over the thick, red hair on Esau's forearm.

"I love both of my sons," said Isaac.

"Yes, I know, Father."

"Yet you have always had a special place in my heart."

"And you in mine, Father."

"I am not long for this world …"

"But, Father …"

"Listen to me, Esau. Let me speak. Take your bow and arrow and go hunt a roebuck. Then come back here and dress the game. Use it to make a venison stew—the kind that you flavor with savory. My favorite. After I have eaten, I will offer you my blessing."

"I would be glad to, Father," said Esau. Then he took his bow and arrow and went off to track down a roebuck.

Rebekah had been in the next room listening to their conversation. Since Jacob was her favorite son, she thought to herself, "I cannot let this happen. If Isaac gives his blessing to Esau, then what will Jacob and I have left?"

Rebekah found Jacob and told him what she had overheard.

"Mother, that is Father's prerogative," Jacob responded. "Besides, there is nothing we can do about it."

"Yes there is, Jacob."

"What?"

"Go out to the fields and kill one of the goats. Find one that has been pasturing on the farther ranges, one that will be tough and taste gamey. I will make the savory stew, and *you* can give it to your father instead of Esau."

"Even if I did that," said Jacob, "Father would know it is me and not Esau."

"I have a plan," said Rebekah. "Now hurry! Go and get the meat before your brother comes back from his hunt."

When Jacob returned with the goat, he helped his mother to skin the animal and dress the meat. She started the stew first, then cleaned the goat's hide and made two sleeves for Jacob to put on. When the stew was cooked, she spooned some into a bowl and brought it to Jacob, along with the goat-hide sleeves.

"Jacob, slip these sleeves over your arms. If your father touches you, he will feel the fur instead of the smooth skin on your arm. Then he will think you are Esau. And here is a set of Esau's clothes so that you will also smell like him."

"What about my voice?" asked Jacob.

"Do the best you can. Now quickly, put these on and take this bowl of stew to your father."

Jacob put on the clothes, pulled up the goat-skin sleeves, and carried the bowl of savory stew into the room where Isaac was lying down.

"Father," he said timidly, "here is your savory."

Isaac awoke from a sleep and asked, "Esau, is that you? Are you back so soon?"

"Yes, Father. It is I, your son. I have brought your savory venison stew."

"Truly, you are a skilled hunter. You must have known exactly where the deer would be at this time of day for you to have hunted one, dressed it, and prepared a stew while I took a short nap."

"With God's help, I was able to do it," Jacob replied.

Isaac sniffed the air and exclaimed, "Oh, yes, it smells delicious. Come, place it on the table next to my bed."

When Isaac heard Jacob putting the bowl of savory stew down onto the table, he reached out quickly and grabbed the boy's arm.

"What? You were always hairier than Jacob, but your arm feels like that of an animal! Perhaps you have been spending too much time out with the wild beasts!" Isaac said, laughing.

Afraid of being discovered, Jacob tried even harder to disguise his voice, but it only caused Isaac to hear how self-conscious he was.

"My eyes have long ago failed me," said Isaac with concern in his voice, "and now it seems that my other senses are also playing tricks on me. Come closer and kiss your old father."

As Jacob bent down and kissed his cheek, Isaac sniffed his son's clothing.

"You smell like Esau, like one who spends his time out in the fresh air and sits by the fire at night. Yet you feel like a wild boar and sound like Jacob does when he has a cold. Is that really you, Esau?"

"It is me, Father, your firstborn son."

"Yes, yes … very well then. Come kneel here by my bed so that I may bless you."

Jacob knelt down, and Isaac placed a wizened hand lightly atop his head.

"May Yahweh give to you and your peoples the riches of the Earth and the wisdom from Heaven to use them wisely. May your house bear fruit for many generations and your heirs number as the grains of sand. That power will flow to you and that others will pay you homage—your brothers, your heirs, descendants of your mother's sons, and the children of other lands. If someone does you harm, may harm be done to them. But to those who bless you, may Yahweh smile upon them."

"Thank you, Father," said Jacob.

"I love you, Esau, my son."

Jacob rose to leave just as Esau came in carrying a bowl of savory venison stew, which he had prepared from the roebuck he had hunted. Without a word he caught Jacob's eyes as his brother walked past him carrying an empty bowl, wearing *his* clothes and a strange set of goat-skin sleeves that smelled of freshly scraped hide.

Esau walked over to his father's bed and asked, "Father, what is going on?"

"Esau," said Isaac, "you are sounding more like your old self again. Have you been cured of your cold so soon?"

"What are you talking about? I have just brought you the savory venison stew that you asked me to prepare."

"Hold out your arm!" Isaac demanded.

Esau rolled up his sleeve and reached out toward his father. Isaac rubbed the hair on the back of his arm.

Isaac opened his mouth as if to speak, but no words came. He turned his head to the side, as if listening for an answer to explain his perplexity. He could tell that Esau was seated next to him—could feel, smell, and hear that this was Esau. Yet he also heard another set of footsteps fading out of the bedroom door toward the kitchen.

"If you are Esau," Isaac cried out, his hands shaking in anger and confusion, "then who was it that I just gave my blessing to?!"

"That was your secondborn son, Jacob."

"What?" yelled Isaac. "Listen to me Esau. Your bother Jacob just deceived me and stole your blessing."

"But you can bless me, too, Father!"

"You know that I cannot! Once my blessing is given, it is given. I cannot take it back and bestow it upon you."

"Father, please! First Jacob took my *bekorah,* my birthright, when I truly offered it to him in jest. Now he has stolen my *berakah,* my blessing, through outright cunning and deceit."

"I have just given to Jacob all the harvests and fruits of the vineyard. I have put your servants at his call and have made him your master," said Isaac sadly.

Tears began to well up in Esau's eyes as he realized the finality of what had just happened. He knelt down beside the bed and pleaded, "I am your firstborn son. Bless me, too, and let me settle things with Jacob."

Isaac withdrew his hand from Esau's, focused his unseeing eyes as if looking into the far distance, and set his mouth grimly.

"Father!" Esau cried. "I love you."

"Esau," replied his father at last. "You are my son. But my heart is now bound by my given word. You can no longer live in the rich lands of Canaan. If you stay here, your brother will rule over you and your descendants. Only by your sword can you now obtain freedom from this burden."

Esau wept in silence, but dark, angry clouds roiled the skies of his inner world. Even as he walked out of his father's bedroom, Esau was hatching a plot to kill Jacob after his father died.

"Out of respect for Mother," he thought, "I will wait until after the period of mourning, then I will take what is rightfully mine."

Esau began to enlist help to carry out his plot against Jacob. Even though his allies were sworn to secrecy, Rebekah soon heard about Esau's schemes.

That very night, she went to Jacob's room and entered. Shaking her beloved son awake, Rebekah said, "Hush, not a sound."

"What is it, Mother?" asked Jacob.

"I have received grave news. Your brother is plotting to kill you so that he can reclaim his *bekorah* and his *berakah.*"

"I can take care of myself," Jacob insisted. "Don't worry."

"No, son, don't be a fool. You stay close to home and are not aware of the standing that your brother has among our people. Many are those who will follow him and share in his wealth, even if he gains it by murdering you."

Hearing the urgency in his mother's voice and swayed by her reason, Jacob agreed. Rebekah helped him to prepare for a swift journey by night.

"I will send word once your brother learns to live with his anger. When Esau comes to see that killing you will solve nothing—only then can you return from Haran."

When the sun next rose upon the house of Isaac in Gerar, no one but Rebekah would know that Jacob had been secreted away to live with the family of his uncle Laban in the land of Haran, in the house of his mother's kin.

Guided by moonlight, Rebekah's last words rang in Jacob's ears as he picked his way along the familiar trails that led far from the only home he had ever known: "May God be with you."

# JACOB, RACHEL, AND LEAH

*Your name shall no longer be Jacob, but Israel,*
*because you strove with God and with men, and prevailed.*

Genesis 32:28

# — 1 —

Rachel had never been just Rachel. She was always Leah's younger sister who wore hand-me-down clothes and had to grind the spices with a pestle while Leah got to use them in the family's cooking. Rachel whiled her days up in the hills where she tended the sheep, while Leah helped around the house and spent half her time primping and preening her long, dark hair.

The fresh air and vigorous work outdoors had sculpted Rachel's lithe legs, her narrow waist, and long, willowy arms that moved with a certain grace that had not gone unnoticed by the men of Haran. Her flaxen hair and hazel eyes were unique among women in her family. Many of her elders believed these attributes were rooted in a long-forgotten ancestor on her mother's side, far to the north.

Often, Rachel awoke before sunrise and hurried down to the well to fill the family's urn. If she got there before anyone else had roiled the water's surface, and when no one was waiting to let their vessel down on the rope to gather water, she could steal a few moments to peer into the glassy surface and see her own reflection at the bottom of the cool, damp hollow. On some mornings, when the light was just so, she saw the curve of her chin, the slightly upturned corners of her mouth and eyes, and the sheen of her thick hair and thought herself pretty. On other days she could hardly bear to look at her reflection; she saw only how the flaws overwhelmed anything that was worthwhile.

In time, Rachel began to realize that her own appearance, and that of other people, had as much to do with how she perceived things on a particular day as it did with what she actually looked like. This freed her to look past the reflection in the pool to what may, or may not, lie beyond. Rachel especially found this to be true with the young men who gathered around the well at midday. Sometimes she made a special trip there to engage their wittiness and attention, while on other days they just seemed crude and immature.

Rachel tied the handle of her jug to the rope that was suspended by a crossbar over the well. Holding the jug upside down, she let it fall into the well where it landed with a hollow *whump*. After the jug had righted itself and filled with water, Rachel pulled up the braided rope, hand over hand, and took hold of the jug's handles. Then she placed the heavy clay vessel on her head and continued her journey up into the hill pastures to water the sheep.

## — 2 —

"Don't be a fool." The words of his mother rang in Jacob's ears as he strode quickly across the plains, up through the hills, and over wide stretches of arid land.

"I am no fool," he thought. "Who has the land? And the birthright? No, I am born to fool, but no fool am I." He stomped through the sand as if using his footfalls to emphasize the words that raced in his thoughts.

With his heart thumping from fear that Esau might be in pursuit, Jacob alternately ran and walked for more than a full day before he stopped to rest for a night. He had traveled swiftly northeast from his birthplace in Gerar toward the house of Laban, his mother's brother, in the city of Paddan-aram in Haran.

The birds and flowers, the grasses and trees, flew past and were of mild interest to him—nothing more than the vaguely familiar land-scape that his father and brother always went on about when telling the stories of their exploits—stories that Jacob always thought must have been greatly embellished. He couldn't imagine that someone who was cut from the same cloth as himself could be capable of such courageous exploits.

After many days of trekking in the wild, Jacob's loneliness grew. "By the time Esau discovers where I have gone," he said aloud to himself, "I will be living in Haran with my new wife. And she will bind me even stronger to the legacy and land of my people. After all, my father always told me to shun the women of Canaan. Both he and

Mother wanted me to take a wife from among the daughters of Uncle Laban."

He could still here his father's words, "God will bless you, as he blessed me, and your grandfather Abraham before me. When you marry into the house of Laban, you will inherit these lands in which you have been raised, which were given to Abraham as a blessing from Yahweh."

"Surely, then, I am not being selfish? I only want those things that are my birthright. This trip is nothing more than a fulfillment of my father's wishes."

On that leg of his journey, Jacob passed through a wide open plain of gently rolling hills. There was little water and the plants that could survive were nothing more than scratch and scrub. After the sun had set, he was at least able to find a small grotto that contained a few rocks and one large boulder for shelter. Unaccustomed to the trials and deprivations of travel in the wilderness, especially when driven with such urgency, Jacob was near exhaustion. He was rationing his food and water and could already see that the soft rolls of flesh around his waist were shrinking. After eating a spare meal and sipping some water, Jacob lay down to sleep and rested his head upon a small rock.

Jacob had slept for some time when he was awakened by something softly touching his cheek. He lay there with eyes still closed and imagined that the wings of a bird had brushed his skin. He opened his eyes and saw a light in the distance. It was not the lingering rouge of sunset, or the blush of early dawn, but a lucid white glow. As he walked toward the light, it grew so bright that it was hard for him to look directly at it. The light was coming from above, from up in the sky, yet it radiated down as if forming a shaft that touched the ground.

Jacob saw that beings were moving up and down the shaft of light, climbing on luminous threads that intertwined to form brilliant cords and veins. One of the beings moved toward Jacob, seeming to float on air. Jacob drew back in fear, but the being moved past him as if it had not noticed his presence. As the being glided, Jacob saw that a pair of enormous wings were working along its back, curving gracefully up and down from the blade of each shoulder. The tips of the wings reached nearly to the being's feet.

Now a light as bright as the sun moved toward Jacob, then hovered by his side where he cowered. Struck by an intense wall of heat, he was suddenly covered with sweat.

"Jacob, son of Isaac, grandson of Abraham, do not fear."

"Please forgive me, my Lord," said Jacob. "Have mercy."

"I have not come to judge you, Jacob. I have come to renew my covenant with the house of Abraham."

"I am your servant," Jacob replied.

"Stand, Jacob, and hear me. No harm will come to you or your people. My hand will protect your house until my promise is fulfilled. One day, your descendants will number as the specks of dust and will be carried by the winds of time to the four directions, north and south, east and west. The land they inhabit will belong to your heirs, who will speak your name as a blessing upon their own people."

At last Jacob stood and shielded his eyes from the light as Yahweh ascended the great heavenly beam, followed by a flock of angels whose feathered wings shimmered with silver light. Then Jacob watched, entranced, until the last angel soared up on Yahweh's celestial illumination.

Now Jacob was overwhelmed with a weariness of spirit. He shivered and closed his eyes, and was instantly lost in a cloak of darkness. When he awoke, Jacob's head lay upon the rock, and the sky was ruddy with the dawn. He rose onto his knees and prayed.

"Yahweh, you have shown me the portal to heaven and your light has entered my soul. Blessed are the angels who came and opened my eyes and ears so that I might see you and hear your words. The majesty of this night, its heavenly glow, has burned a mark of faith on my soul. As surely as you promise to be by my side and provide for my people, I will one day return to the house of my father and will pledge to you one-tenth of everything from all that I receive. Here, where your presence came before me, I will make an altar in honor of your name."

Jacob built an altar of the stones he gathered from that place. On top of the altar, he placed the stone on which he had rested his head. When it was finished, he anointed the altar with oil.

"Here, Yahweh, is an altar to mark the place where you showed me a beth El, a house of God, the gate of heaven."

Having no freshly killed animal to make a blood sacrifice, Jacob took some of his last remaining dried meat and placed it on the altar.

The rising sun saw Jacob continue along the road to Haran. But now, although tired and hungry, he moved with a purpose and conviction that he had never felt before his vision at beth El.

"I see my life clearly, now," he reflected. "Everything I have done up to this time, I have done for myself. But now I have witnessed a host of angels. Yahweh has appeared and renewed the pledge with me and my people. How could I have been so blind! It has taken me this long to finally understand my place in the lineage. What a fool!"

# — 3 —

Jacob continued toward the east. He traveled across the last of the arid lands on the outskirts of Haran. When he came to the top of the next rise he looked out across a rolling expanse of pasture dotted with sheep. He climbed over a wall and walked toward a place in the distance where several large flocks were gathered, emanating the familiar scents of lanolin and dung.

The sheep parted, as Jacob approached several shepherds who were gathered around a large well.

"Welcome, stranger!" they said. "We have been waiting for you."

"Greetings," Jacob replied. "How could you have heard that I was coming?"

"No, no, my friend," said one of the shepherds, "not you, exactly, just one more person to help us move the heavy capstone off the mouth of this well. The three of us were not quite enough to do it."

"Gladly," offered Jacob, "if I may also partake."

"Of course."

The four men encircled the large stone that covered the well. On signal, they strained together and carefully lifted the stone, sliding it off to the side. After each had taken a long drink, they began to bring water to their flocks. Jacob worked alongside the shepherds.

"Are we very far from Haran?" Jacob asked one of the shepherds.

"Not at all," said one. "Do you have business there?"

"I am looking for my uncle and his family."

"And who is that?"

"Do you know Laban?"

"You mean Nahor's son?"

"Yes!" replied Jacob. "You know them?"

"Everybody knows them. Nahor is a prominent member of this town, and he is quite wealthy. There, that is the last of the sheep. Let's go help the others move the stone back over the well."

As Jacob and the shepherd walked toward the well, they saw that a lovely young woman had arrived to water her flock. Jacob froze, shook the shoulder of the shepherd, and asked quietly, "Who is that young woman? She has a face like an angel!"

"You mean Rachel?" answered the shepherd. "Yes, she is lovely, I suppose. I have known her my whole life. We have tended sheep together in these hills since we were children."

"And you have not asked for her hand?"

"No, no, my friend. She is like a sister to me."

"Tell me about her," insisted Jacob.

"She is from the very house you were just asking about. Rachel is the daughter of your uncle Laban."

"Please, introduce me, but do not tell her who I am."

When Jacob reached the well, he and the shepherd walked over to greet Rachel.

"Good day, Rachel," said the shepherd.

"And to you, Tabor," Rachel replied.

"Here, meet a newcomer to these parts," said the shepherd. "His name is Jacob."

"Greetings," said Rachel.

"It is my pleasure," Jacob said in reply. "I could help you to water your flock, if you like."

"Would you? That would be kind. It is a bit late in the day to start the watering, and I want to get the flock back to a safe pasture before dark."

As they watered the flock, Jacob asked Rachel about the weather. He inquired what it was like to live in Haran. But he was so taken by her stunning appearance—her burnished hair, the slight golden tint in the glint of her eyes—that he hardly heard a word she said. After the sheep had all been watered, they returned to help slide the capstone back into place.

Rachel said goodbye to the other shepherds and turned toward Jacob. But before she could bid farewell, he stepped forward, took her head gently between his hands, and kissed her passionately.

She yielded just a trifle, then pulled back and said with equal passion, "Sir!"

"I am so happy!" he said as tears streamed down his face.

"You are a strange man!"

"I am Jacob, the son of Rebekah, your father's sister."

"Why didn't you tell me when we met?"

"You are so beautiful … I couldn't take my eyes off of … I mean … I wasn't thinking! As soon as I saw you, all I wanted to do was be by your side and help you water the sheep."

"Well, come then, come back to our house. My father and mother will be glad to meet you. This is wonderful!"

Rachel led Jacob down out of the hills and into the city of Paddan-aram. Merchants were selling their wares in the narrow streets. As they walked past, one vendor held out a hand that was filled with delicious-looking treats.

"Dates, almonds, carob!" someone called. "Here, taste these pistachios. They are the finest in the city."

"Almonds, walnuts, figs!" cried another. The luxuriant smell of roasting nuts and the alluring aroma of baked sweets that were new to Jacob made him realize that he was famished.

Despite his infatuation with Rachel, the vendors reminded Jacob of the custom to bring a gift of food when visiting. He stopped at one of the market carts to purchase some dates and figs wrapped in broad palm leaves as a gift for his uncle Laban.

When they neared Laban's house, Jacob took Rachel's hand and pulled her to a stop. "Perhaps I should wait here while you go to your father to tell him who is coming and to explain how we met at the well."

"What?" said Rachel in mock surprise. "Are you suddenly shy? You were not so cautious at the well, as I recall!"

"This is different."

"Oh? And how is that?"

"Laban is your father."

"Don't worry," she said, smiling, as she touched him on the shoulder. "If you made it across the desert, I think you can survive the journey over our doorstep!"

## — 4 —

"Father!" Rachel called as she led Jacob into the house. "There is someone here to meet you, and he has come a long way."

Laban entered the front room and walked over to Jacob. He was wearing a heavy, lustrous robe with gold embroidery that Jacob thought handsome, but far too heavy for the heat of the day.

"Father, this is Jacob, whom I met at the well."

"And ..." said Laban as he stared coldly at Jacob.

"Perhaps, Father, you will notice the family resemblance. I think he has his mother's eyes."

Laban stared at Jacob for some time. As he waited, Jacob wiped away the beads of sweat that had begun to form on his forehead.

"Hmmm, I do know those eyes," Laban puzzled. "But it has been many years since I have had the pleasure of my sister Rebekah's company. Could this possibly be my nephew, Jacob, come all this way?"

"It is I, Uncle," said Jacob as he bowed and offered Laban the parcel of dates and figs.

"Welcome, Jacob!" Laban said gladly as he received the gift. Then he threw his big arms around his nephew, enfolding him in the heavy robe, tinged with the sour smell of sweat. When Laban finally stepped back to look at Jacob he gestured behind him.

"Please, here is my wife, your aunt Tamar, and here is my other daughter, Leah."

Jacob embraced each woman in turn, kissing both cheeks. As he pulled his face away from that of Leah, she could see that he was staring at Rachel, who was standing behind her. As soon as Leah saw the look in Jacob's eyes and turned to see his gaze being returned in kind by Rachel, Leah knew that they were in love. But Leah *knew* that she must be the first to marry. She also believed that her own beauty and refinement would be able to win Jacob over from her pale shepherdess of a sister.

"Come now nephew," said Laban. "Sit and tell us of your journey. It must have taken something very important to bring you all this way."

"Yes, Uncle," Jacob began, and he recalled the entire story of how he had come to Haran.

Jacob told of his episode with Isaac and Esau and of his journey across the arid lands to find Haran. When he was finished, he looked at Laban and Tamar and said, "May I now speak to you, Aunt and Uncle, in private?"

Tamar looked over at Leah and Rachel and made a gesture with her eyes. The two young women left the room and walked outside.

"Most of all, Uncle Laban and Aunt Tamar, it has always been my father's wish, when I was old enough to marry, that I would return to the house of my mother's brother to find a wife."

"You are welcome to stay in our house as long as you like," offered Laban, somewhat tepidly. Then he turned and cast a cautious glance at Tamar—a look that told her he was wary of their artful nephew.

That night as Jacob unpacked his belongings, he noticed a faint smell of cinnamon on his hands where they had touched Rachel's neck. As his nose lingered there, he relived the kiss they had shared.

In the satchel that his mother had quickly prepared for him when he was leaving home back in Gerar, Jacob discovered a small bundle hidden under his food, clothes, and other necessities. He reached down and felt the course hair of camel. He pulled up the bundle and recognized it immediately.

Although he did not withdraw the object from its case, he held it in his hand. For the first time in his life, Jacob began to appreciate what it symbolized. He thought of how his grandfather Abraham, and his father, Isaac, had struggled, fought, and worked to keep the covenant with Yahweh. "Here, in my hand tonight, I am holding the symbol of my people's history."

At that moment, Jacob reflected on what he had done to trick his father and again heard the anguished cries of Esau when he found he had been deceived. Tears welled up in his eyes. He fell down on his knees.

"Yahweh, forgive me. I pray only that I prove worthy in your eyes."

One day, after Jacob had been living in his uncle's household for one turn of the moon, Laban approached him after the evening meal.

"Jacob, you have been helpful in many ways since you arrived— aiding with the shepherding, assisting me with my business and in other ways, as you can—but surely you did not come to live in my house and work here indefinitely."

"Uncle, I am relieved that you have brought up the subject, for there is something that I want very much."

"What is that?"

"I am in love with Rachel and would ask you for her hand in marriage."

"That is as I suspected," said Laban, with a smile that was barely masked. "But Leah is my eldest, and she is to marry before Rachel will wed."

"Please, Uncle, tell me what I must do to have Rachel's hand in marriage."

"Continue to work for me as you have for a time, and I will see how serious you are about your feelings for her, and I would know that this is not a passing fancy."

"How long would you have me stay here and work for you?"

"Seven years."

Jacob sat in shocked silence for some time. He glanced at his uncle Laban, whose eyes were fixed on his, unflinching. Finally, Jacob looked directly at Laban and said, "If that is what you wish, Uncle, then I will do it. For I dearly love Rachel."

———

That evening, Jacob took a long walk through the city streets and wandered out to the well where he had first met Rachel. Alone in that place, with the stars overhead, he kneeled by the stones that ringed the well and prayed.

"Yahweh, now is my chance to show that I am worthy of your covenant. I will honor my agreement to live here in Paddan-aram for seven years and work for my uncle Laban. Then I will marry Rachel and begin a family."

# — 5 —

Seven years is a long time to wait when you are in love. At times, Jacob was beside himself with desire for Rachel. In spite of how the time seemed to drag, Jacob was good to his word. He worked hard for Laban—helping with his customers, going to marketplace, learning how to keep the accounts. Jacob learned enough to know that his uncle was holding back some of his wages and paying him far less than he was worth.

"When the time comes for you to marry Rachel," Laban would say, "you will make a fine merchant."

Being in love can also cause seven years to fly. Rachel saw her betrothed every day at the evening meal. Although they were allowed to speak to each other when other members of the family were present, they had no time alone.

Rachel watched Jacob closely. "Jacob is a good man," she told her friends. "He is learning my father's business so quickly! The other night, I heard them talking about how Jacob had found a buyer for some of the finest, most expensive fabric that my father purchases from the East."

"But do you love him?" they would ask. And for a long time, she didn't answer.

Then one day Rachel responded, "Yes, I do love him."

"Tell us!" demanded her friends.

"It is like a small candle that has grown brighter and burned hotter with each passing moon. Sometimes, I fear it is going to consume me. Then I remind myself of what my mother says: 'Rachel, my dear, all good things are worth waiting for.'"

Throughout that time, Leah took every opportunity to be close to Jacob and to do small favors for him. Jacob, in turn, always tried to be warm and kind to Leah, believing that these gestures would endear him all the more to Rachel. But with such a strong faith in her own powers of attraction, Leah mistook Jacob's attentions for something more than was intended.

When the seven years were nearly over, Rachel's father went to her and said, "Daughter, your wedding is fast approaching."

"Yes, Father, I know."

"Since you have been living in the same house as Jacob, but not as husband and wife, we are going to send you to your aunt's in the city of Gozan for a week and a day. It is an old custom for the betrothed to take time away from her intended before the wedding— a time for reflection on the sacred covenant she is about to enter into."

"As you wish, Father. I have waited seven years. What is one more week? The wedding will be all the more wonderful."

"But you must not tell Jacob exactly where you are going, or for how long you will be away. It is all part of the mystery."

"Yes, Father."

That same day, after Rachel had been escorted from Haran to the house of her aunt in Gozan, Laban sat down with Jacob after the evening meal.

"Nephew, you have worked hard for these seven years. You have more than earned the right to be given Rachel's hand in marriage as I promised."

"Uncle, being patient has not been easy."

"Yes, I know, Son. I have seen that in you."

"What are the customs in your house to prepare for the wedding?" asked Jacob.

"As you know, Rachel has been sent away for seclusion, to live with an aunt for a time."

"Yes, she told me the generalities. She also said she could tell me no more."

"In exactly one week's time, Rachel will return for your wedding day. Following the ceremony, the festivities will last for a week. We will spare no expense. It will be glorious!"

"Uncle, I cannot thank you enough."

"You have worked hard and earned all of it, and then some," Laban assured him.

Jacob thought, "I'm well aware of that, too."

On the morning of the wedding, Laban pulled Jacob aside and spoke to him in a solemn voice. "Jacob, hear me now. We have a strict custom in our family that is practiced by all newlyweds from the morning of their wedding day until the next sunrise."

"I'm listening, Uncle. What is the custom?"

"In order to preserve the sanctity of the marriage vow, and to allow the newlyweds to experience the full spiritual nature of their union, the bride and bridegroom do not speak a word to each other from sunrise to sunrise. No matter what happens on your wedding night, Rachel will remain veiled and not a single word shall pass between you."

"Uncle, I had no idea that your family was so sentimental. I don't care whether we speak or not. I just want to be with Rachel and to share our love."

"So be it," said Laban.

The ceremony was to take place in the evening, jeweled with a sea of candles and spangled by the starlit sky. When all of the guests had assembled, Jacob and his bride were led to the altar. Jacob, who had spent much of his life around the women of his house and that of his uncle, was surprised to find his legs shaking with nerves. He saw that Rachel, hidden beneath her veil, seemed as calm as a limpid pool of water.

Before Jacob realized what had happened, their vows had been exchanged and the wedding blessed. Soon the festivities were winding down. It had been a whirlwind evening of delicious food, exotic music, and vessels of sweet-scented, sumptuous wine. Then Jacob saw his uncle Laban approaching.

"Well, my children," said Laban throwing his arms around the newlyweds. "We will take good care of the guests. If you were both to disappear into the night, who would know?"

Jacob and his bride walked slowly to the ornate wedding tent, which had been erected a good distance from the crowd. Once inside, Jacob was overflowing with words of longing and devotion—feelings that he had been unable to give voice to for seven years! But he remembered the custom that his uncle had asked him to honor.

"She is wearing the perfume that I have never smelled on anyone but Rachel," he thought, "that floral essence that she makes herself and infuses with a touch of cinnamon."

He recalled their first passionate kiss by the well seven years past. Yet, now, on their wedding night, his bride seemed hesitant, even languid.

"Perhaps it is just as well," he thought. "I have drunk so much wine that sleep will soon overtake me."

The next morning Jacob awoke to see the intricate designs painted onto the walls of the tent, backlit by the first rays of sun. "At long last," he thought, "I awake next to my beloved."

He looked at his bride, still asleep, her veil slightly askew and fluttering gently with each breath. Jacob reached over and slowly lifted the veil. He caught his breath and said aloud, "What! Leah? How did you get into my bed? What are you doing here?"

Leah sat bolt upright and gasped. Then she remembered everything. "Jacob, please do not yell. Don't be angry with me."

"Are you mad? Don't be angry with you? What did you do, switch places with Rachel in the middle of the night? Is this some kind of trick?"

"You mean Uncle didn't tell you?"

"Tell me what?"

"That you were going to marry me instead of Rachel."

"But … no … it was Rachel yesterday. That was her wedding dress and her perfume …"

"It's what they told me to wear," said Leah. "And we borrowed a bit of Rachel's perfume. I didn't think she would mind."

"Didn't think she would mind that you switched places with her and married me instead? I can't believe you have done this!"

"Calm down, Jacob."

"No, I will not calm down. I am going to talk to Uncle Laban this instant!"

After Jacob had confronted his uncle, who listened with a calm and even disposition, Laban said, "Jacob, you are right to be angry. But you know that it is a custom among our people that the elder sister must first marry before the younger."

"How could you do this to me, Uncle, after I lived and worked at your side for seven years. Is it also a custom that one man should keep his word and the other should break his?"

"Jacob, I see that you don't understand."

"Understand what?!"

"I have not broken my word."

"What are you saying?"

"Rachel will come back this morning. She knows nothing of what has happened. When she arrives, we will tell her. Then, whatever happens will be in your hands, both of you."

"Surely, you don't mean …"

"Ah, Jacob, you are beginning to understand. I have not broken my pledge to you. Today is exactly seven years since we made our agreement. On this day I offer you the hand of my second daughter. Everything is still in place for your wedding to Rachel this evening."

There was a long silence while Jacob began to see the extraordinary situation that he was in. "You mean, Uncle, that you would have me marry *both* your daughters?"

"Yes, but only if you agree to do an equal measure of work for Leah."

"Another seven years?" asked Jacob incredulously.

"There it is," Laban replied.

Jacob got up and went out for a long walk into the countryside. The longer he walked, the more anxious he became to return to the house of Laban to marry his true love.

That same morning, when Rachel returned from her aunt's house in Gozan, she was excited to see how beautifully the family's yard had been prepared for her wedding.

"Mother, Father, I am home," she called as she stepped inside.

"Come here dear," said her mother earnestly. "I have something to tell you."

"Is everything all right?" asked Rachel.

"Well, yes … and … no," replied Tamar.

The two women entered Rachel's bedroom. In a short while, servants out in the courtyard heard Rachel scream, "No, Mother! Please tell me it is not so!" Without another word, Rachel stormed out of her bedroom.

"Rachel, wait!" her mother called after her.

Tears streaming down her face, she walked briskly through the streets of Paddan-aram, ignoring greetings from friends and members of her large family as she strode past. Rachel had no idea where her feet were carrying her. She only knew that she wanted to get as far away from her own house and her duplicitous family as she could be. Soon, she found herself leaning out over the water that she used for the sheep, tears falling with a hollow sound inside the well.

A hand gently touched Rachel on the shoulder. "Go away, Mother!" she yelled. "Why did you follow me here?"

"Rachel," said a familiar voice. "It is me."

She straightened up and turned to see Jacob standing there.

"How could you?" she screamed, beating her fists against his chest.

Jacob grabbed her wrists and held them. "Rachel, my love, I didn't know. Your family told me of this custom of secrecy and how the married couple couldn't see each other or speak on their first night. They dressed Leah in your wedding gown, and she wore your perfume. I thought it was you!"

"And you couldn't tell it wasn't me?"

"There *was* something wrong, something missing, but I thought you were just afraid because it was our first night together."

"But what does it matter now," said Rachel. "You're married, and it can't be undone."

"No, it can't. But I love *you*. I don't love your sister. Please don't abandon everything we've waited so long for. None of this was our fault, nor was it our design."

Jacob released Rachel's wrists, and her arms fell by her sides in resignation, but not in defeat. Slowly, Jacob pulled her toward him and embraced the only woman he had ever loved.

"I cannot change what has happened," said Jacob. "But I will do whatever you ask of me now. If you can still find it in your heart, I want nothing more than to become your husband—tonight."

Rachel was wise enough to know that there are moments— mostly uninvited—when everything that will happen for the rest of one's life hangs in a balance that can be tipped by a single word, or by peering into someone's eyes a certain way. Almost imperceptibly, Jacob could feel her arms sliding up his back, until her hands were clasped behind him.

Bringing her mouth up to his ear, in a voice that Jacob could barely hear, Rachel whispered—no, breathed—"I have loved you since that day seven years ago when I saw you standing by this very well. I was yours from that first kiss. Even if our life will not be what we had hoped because of what has happened, I will always love you, and from this day on as your wife."

Neither Rachel, Jacob, nor Leah could have imagined what lay ahead.

## — 6 —

After her wedding, Rachel found herself in a position of favor above that of her sister Leah for the first time in her life. Jacob was smitten with Rachel. He spent almost all his free time with her and bestowed every sentiment of love upon the woman he had waited and worked for seven long years to marry.

"Rachel, my dear, how I have missed you!" Jacob said when he returned from another day of working with Laban. Then, in the next breath, "Leah, what have you made us to eat? It smells delicious."

At first, Leah understood and accepted her situation. In order to marry Jacob, she had tacitly deceived both him and her sister. Leah had secretly and vainly hoped, "When I prove my love to Jacob, he will also come to love me." As time passed, however, and things did not change, Leah began to see how her heart's desires had blinded her to reality: how time can just as easily grow the sharp thorns of the cactus as it can unfurl the blossoms of the lily. After months of enduring the emotional jabs and slights that come with being the second wife, she was beginning to feel more than a little prickly.

One evening, when no one else was home, she walked into the garden and prayed. "Yahweh, how long must I go on atoning for my dishonesty? Jacob would love me if only I could bear him a son. Please, forgive me and have mercy."

Within the turn of one moon, Leah's prayers were answered, and she conceived. When the child was born, and Leah saw that Yahweh had heard her plea, she named her first son Reuben, "he has seen my distress." Leah would soon learn how closely Yahweh had listened and how dearly he took her prayers to heart. In rapid succession, Leah gave birth to three more sons, naming them Simeon, "God has heard," Levi, "he will cling," and Judah, "I shall praise."

That is how it began. While the men were out bargaining with other merchants and fighting the battles of a wider world, Leah laid down the gauntlet of the heirs. Each newborn became an innocent pawn in a rancorous dance of marital thrusts and parries—the battle of the babies.

With each passing year, burdened by a growing family, the constant needs of children, and an often pregnant Leah, Jacob had less and less time for Rachel. Every new child was a painful reminder to Rachel that she could not conceive, not matter how often she and Jacob tried. When she protested that he hardly ever spent time with her, Jacob would say, "You know how much I love you, but there is so much to do and so little time in each day. I have a large family to feed now." Bit by bit, Rachel saw her role in Jacob's life, and the passionate love they once shared, fading like the withered petals of the hyssop blossom—once white and warmly scented, now dried and lifeless underfoot.

Out of desperation and fear, Rachel went to Jacob and said, "I cannot live if I don't have a child."

"Do I look like God?" he answered.

"Don't be cruel, Jacob."

He took her in his arms and said, "I am sorry, love. But there is nothing more I can do."

"I have a proposition. Take one of my slave girls—the one named Bilhah—take her as your wife. That way I can give you a child."

Out of love for Rachel, Jacob agreed. Bilhah did conceive and had a son.

Holding the child for the first time, Rachel said, "I will name you Dan, 'he has given me justice.'"

Meanwhile, Leah's run of conceptions had stopped. She resented the attention that Jacob once again showered upon Rachel and her new son, Dan.

"He is not really your flesh and blood!" she would say in the heat of anger.

"You have four sons now," Rachel replied. "What would it take to satisfy you?"

Less than a year later, the slave girl Bilhah had a second son by Jacob. The relationship between the two sisters had become so bitter that Rachel named the poor boy Naphtali, "I have fought."

Leah struck back. Because she had stopped conceiving, she gave a slave girl named Zilpah to Jacob to become his fourth wife. In time, Zilpah had a son that Leah, feeling blessed, named Gad, "good luck."

A year later, Zilpah gave birth to another son. With six sons now, Leah was delighted and felt that, surely, she was seen as happy in the eyes of other women. So this new child was called Asher, "my happiness."

Meanwhile, down in the bazaar, where the merchants gathered, and where Jacob was well known, his nickname had become "busy man."

"The coneys have nothing over him!" men would say. "In the time that it takes most of us to have a child, Jacob produces a litter!"

As the number of children grew, the rivalry between Rachel and Leah only intensified. One day, Reuben found a patch of mandrakes growing amid the wheat. He picked an armful and brought them to his mother, Leah. He had heard that the plant was an aphrodisiac, and he thought it might help Leah in her quest to attract the attentions of Jacob. Rachel happened to be visiting at the time.

"Please, Leah, may I have those mandrakes?"

"And what will you give me in return? Isn't it enough that Jacob spends almost all his nights with you?"

"I will make a trade," Rachel replied. "Give me the mandrakes, and I will make sure that Jacob comes to you tonight."

That evening when Jacob returned home, he said, "What is that interesting scent? It is rich—very appealing."

"Those are the mandrakes that I got from Leah today,"

"She picked them and *gave* them to you?"

"Not exactly. Reuben picked them."

"And how did you get them?"

"I traded with Leah."

"For what?"

"She said she would give them to me if you would agree to be with her tonight."

A short time after Leah and Rachel traded their man for a mandrake, Rachel saw that her gambit had failed when she learned that Leah had again conceived. When this child was born, and Leah thought about how she had paid for the evening with Jacob, she named the boy Issachar, "wages."

Already well ahead of Rachel with the number of heirs she had produced, Leah went on to have two more children with Jacob. After their seventh boy was born, Leah at last believed that the race had been won by the prolific—that Jacob would hold her in high regard. This child she named, Zebulun, "he will respect me." Leah's seventh and last child with Jacob was a girl that she named Dinah.

Leah's fecundity caused Rachel to obsess. Although the slave girl Bilhah had given her two sons by Jacob, Rachel was at times despondent over being unable to bear a child. Day after day, as she failed to conceive, her prayers took on a tone of desperation. At last, Yahweh granted Rachel her heart's desire. When the first child she bore came into the world, she was still wishing for another, so she named him Joseph, "may he add."

One day, soon after Joseph's birth, Jacob pulled himself away from his family and took a quiet walk to a height of land that looked out over the valley of Haran. There he prayed. "Yahweh, I am eternally grateful for the children you have brought into my family and especially for Joseph, my first child with Rachel. Out in the desert long ago, when the angels appeared and you promised that my descendants would one day number as the specks of dust, I did not think you meant it would come to pass in one generation!"

## — 7 —

Now that his own family had grown into an ample brood, Jacob turned his attention to the breeding of kids and lambs.

"Uncle Laban," he said one day, "I have worked for you for nearly twenty years. Your house has grown wealthy, and Yahweh has blessed me with a large family. Now it is time for me to return to my own country, to go home with the wives and children that I have rightfully earned."

"How much do you want?" asked Laban.

Jacob was keenly aware that for many years Laban had been cheating him out of the wages he was due and that they could never agree to a sum that would make up for what he had already lost. But Jacob had a plan.

"Uncle, I won't even ask for wages. You have large flocks of the whitest sheep and the blackest goats because I have bred them wisely. These animals are the envy of all your neighbors."

"And ..."

"Let me take only the inferior black sheep and the ugly spotted goats to build my own flocks and herds. Then, when I am ready, I will go to my people."

"As you wish, Jacob. That sounds fair." But Laban was thinking, "You fool."

Laban was unaware that he was about to learn the painful lessons of Abimelech, the reluctant benefactor of Jacob's father, Isaac.

With his deal in hand, Jacob was back on familiar ground. He had already worked his wit, now he plied his wisdom, for he was an expert in the ways of animal husbandry. Jacob led all of Laban's animals on a three-day journey from their house. Each night along the way, he stopped and prayed, "Yahweh, please bless me in my work, for my father-in-law has paid me none of the wages that are rightfully mine."

"Jacob," answered Yahweh, "you have worked hard and upheld the covenant we entered into at beth El. Go to the distant fields, breed the sheep and goats. There with the birth of each black sheep and every striped and spotted goat, I will give you the wages that you justly deserve."

"God, I have honored my pledge. Why has the path you have set before me been so tortured?"

"Jacob, when you hide beneath the skin of another animal, how is anyone to know your heart? The path you have taken to reach your destiny is the one you have chosen."

Patiently and with great care, Jacob bred his new flock from several generations of Laban's pure white sheep and lustrous black goats. Each time a black sheep was born, Jacob carefully bred it with one of the best white sheep in the flock. When one of these pairings gave birth to a black sheep, he waited until it was mature and again bred it with the strongest in the flock. After several generations, Jacob had a sizeable herd of black sheep that were strong, well formed, and bore thick wool.

Using the same technique with the herd of goats, he bred each of the striped and spotted goats with the best among the black animals. Within three generations, Jacob's herd of mottled goats was every bit as robust as Laban's black one. In time, by breeding and trading well, Jacob built up his flocks and herds. He also traded some of his animals for donkeys, camels, and slaves.

Jacob often watched the wolves that haunted the edges of his flocks and herds. After many years of seeing the results of their attacks on his animals, the howls that once raised his hair in fear he now heard as nothing more than threats to the source of his livelihood. He tried offering the wolves the sheep and goats that died of illness or injury by placing the remains out in the open away from the flock. When there were no dead animals to offer, the wolves returned. He tried killing them with his bow, but they soon learned to stay beyond the range of arrows.

One morning, Jacob followed some wolf tracks back to a den where he discovered an abandoned pup whose mother had been killed in a fight with a rival. The pup came ambling over to him, and he could see that it was a female.

"Where is your mother, little one?" asked Jacob as he picked it up. "You won't survive another day without someone to look after you."

Under Jacob's care, the pup grew into one of the largest wolves he had ever seen. He simply named it She-wolf. Separated from its kind, She-wolf imprinted on the flock and seem to believe that she, too, was a sheep. As She-wolf grew, Jacob saw the irony in how fiercely his new ally fought against her own kind to protect the flock.

After years of living out in the open with his animals and of see-ing the world through She-wolf's eyes, Jacob finally understood why his father, Isaac, and brother, Esau, held such a deep appreciation for all things wild.

## — 8 —

Every time Jacob left the flocks and spent a night at Laban's house, he secreted something of his belongings back to the tent where he lived near the animals. One small piece at a time, he was preparing for when his family would leave.

Laban's sons became suspicious. "Why is Jacob fielding the sheep and goats so far from some of our best pasture?" they asked. They spied on Jacob and began to suspect that he was somehow cheating Laban.

"Uncle," they said, "Jacob is producing great flocks of thickly fleeced black sheep and strong herds of well-muscled spotted goats. You own flocks are being neglected."

Rachel and Leah began to hear what their brothers were saying to Laban. They told Jacob the news, and he said, "Yahweh has told me to leave this land and return to the home of my people. Now let us make haste."

Rachel and Leah spent that night at the house of Tamar and Laban. They each packed up a small bundle containing their essentials and their most precious keepsakes. Rachel stole the small statues that marked her family's lineage and to whose owner the riches of their household would be handed down. When the two sisters left the next morning, their parents suspected nothing.

Jacob and his wives, servants, and slaves herded the sheep and goats to the south and west, forded the Euphrates River, and continued west toward Mount Gilead.

The first night they stopped to rest, Rachel asked, anxiously, "Do you think they will find us soon?"

"It will not be difficult to track a herd of goats, a flock of sheep, and the hoofprints of a hundred camels," Jacob said.

Laban did not discover that Jacob and his family were gone until three days after they had razed their tents and begun the journey. When he was finally told the news, Laban was furious.

"Prepare your camels and take only the necessities," Laban said to his brothers. "We must move quickly to catch up with Jacob and my daughters."

It was the dry season, and the camels raised billowing clouds of dust. Hundreds of cloven hooves thundered across the vast open spaces and forded the shallows of the Euphrates. Laban and his brothers drove their camels hard across the land as if they were a small invading army pursuing a murderous thief.

After three days of enduring camel spit and dust, Laban remarked, "I don't see how such a large group could move so far in this amount of time. They cannot be more than a day's journey ahead of us."

That night, in a dream, Yahweh said to Laban, "When you find Jacob and his wives, hold your tongue."

Seven days into their journey, the pursuers caught up with Jacob in the foothills. After waiting on the slopes of Mount Gilead for the night, Laban and his men entered the camp of Jacob and his family.

As Laban neared their tents, he drew his sword and pointed it at Jacob. The blade gleamed.

"Would you kill the husband of your two daughters and the father of these children right in front of them?" asked Jacob.

Seeing a threat to her master, She-wolf exploded out from behind a tent and tore across the encampment toward Laban.

"She-wolf, stop!" called Jacob. The animal halted in its tracks but continued to snarl at Laban.

With a watchful eye upon the beast, a newly chastened Laban said, "These animals are stolen!"

"Open your eyes, Uncle. Do you see a single sheep that is not black? One goat that is not spotted? I have taken only the inferior animals, as we agreed."

"This is some kind of trick. These animals are not small and weak as those of their color normally are. They are healthy and robust—in fact, some of the best I have seen."

"That proves only that I know how to breed well."

Looking over at Jacob's wives and the horde of children sheltered behind them, Laban said, "Your ability to breed has never been in doubt."

"Mock me and you mock your own flesh and blood!" said Jacob, drawing his own sword. She-wolf's growls grew more menacing.

Again, looking warily at the wolf, Laban said, "If you are innocent, why did you flee my homeland like a thief and take my daughters as if they were your hostages? After twenty years of living in my house, you said goodbye to no one. We would have given you a proper sendoff, a celebration with music and a feast."

"You have paid me scant sums for the years of work I have done," Jacob protested. "And still you act as if the things I have earned are rightfully yours. If I had told you I was going, you would have made certain that I left with very little to my name, perhaps even forbidding your daughters to come with me."

"Very well. Even if you have been merely a deceiver, and not a thief, we will not leave here without the family heirlooms. They are the vessels of our lineage, and they belong to us!"

"What are you talking about?" asked Jacob. His eyes wandered over to Leah, who looked him in the eye, quizzically, and shrugged her shoulders. When Jacob turned to look for Rachel, he did not see her.

Jacob walked over to Laban and gestured toward the tents. "Search as you will, for I have nothing to hide."

Without a word, Laban and his brothers began a careful search through every bedroll, wrap of provisions, and satchel. They combed the tents of Jacob and Leah and of the slave girls Zilpah and Bilhah.

Laban entered Rachel's tent and found her seated on a bedroll in which she was hiding the family heirlooms. She remained sitting.

"Daughter, will you not come to greet me?"

Drawing upon a guise that she knew would not fail, especially in the eyes of a man, Rachel said, "Father, I am glad to see you. Please do not be upset. I am having my time in a woman's moon, and I cannot stand."

Laban stared at Rachel for an instant before he realized what she meant. "Oh, yes, I see," he said sheepishly. "Of course, stay where you are. I will search the tent quickly and be gone."

When the camp had been searched, Laban and his brothers gathered back where Jacob was still waiting.

"Nothing." Laban said. "We found nothing."

"Yes, Uncle, you have found the end of my patience," Jacob said, his voice rising. "For twenty years you have begrudged me a pittance of pay for the hard work I gave you and your animals. Your flock is the strongest in Paddan-aram because of the care and the fine breeding they have received for all that time. Through cold nights and blistering days, I tended your animals, driving away the wolves and jackals under the stars while you slept safely in your bed! I have taken only what I have earned and am traveling with my family to the land of my fathers. Now you chase me down like a fugitive and insult me by searching my belongings. And for what? For nothing."

"One day, Jacob, when your sons and daughters marry and leave your household, you will understand. In my eyes, they are still my family. These are my lands and my animals that you have driven away from my pastures. But I can see now that this is the way of the past. It is time for us to make amends."

A large flat stone lay close to where they were standing. Jacob picked up another stone and placed it upon the slab. He stood and gestured toward Laban, who understood. Laban then carried a stone and placed it next to Jacob's. Their two families worked together to build a tall tapered cairn on that place.

Then Jacob motioned toward the stones and said, "We will name this Galeed, 'cairn of witness.'" From that day on, that place has been known as Mount Gilead.

"In my native Aramaic," said Laban, an Armenian, "we say 'Jegar-sahadutha.'"

"It will also be called 'Mizpah,'" added Jacob. "For this stone will be the watchpost between our people. I will never pass this stone to attack you or your kin. And you will always leave me and my family in peace while we remain on this side of the stone," said Jacob, pointing to the south and west.

"Agreed," replied Laban, "in the eyes of the God of Abraham and Nahor."

"And the God of Isaac," said Jacob.

That evening, Jacob sacrificed a sheep, and they prepared a meal for everyone. Leah brought her lyre from the tent and began to play. Under the shimmering stars they sang to Leah's music. On into the night they shared the old family stories, their clothing rich with the aromas of smoke and mutton stew. One of Jacob's servants began to play a drum. The sound pealed like thunder and rolled down the passes between the hills.

Late in the evening, when the music and percussion had subsided and eyelids were growing heavy, Rachel emerged from her tent and sat down among them, staring at the fire. The children walked over and settled, cross-legged, in a circle at her feet. She-wolf came and flopped down in their midst. As the youngest ones petted her thick fur, squeals of delight rippled through the darkness.

# — 9 —

The long, swift journey of seven days, followed by the stress of Laban's unexpected confrontation and the exertion of his visit, left Jacob and his family tired and in need of rest. Seeing this, Jacob said, "We will stay another day and night here at Galeed. Let us be ready to leave tomorrow morning."

That evening, Jacob walked alone into the wilds to clear his mind, to escape for a time the burden of being responsible for the well-being of so many people and to shed the frustrations of dealing with marital rivalries and the strain of having in-laws who would chase him halfway across the desert, just to accuse him of being a thief.

Years of tending sheep and goats, of sleeping under the spangled sky dome and listening to the many voices of the wind, had opened Jacob's eyes to the beauty of the land he lived in. Jacob's love of nature had deepened in his spirit, had grown into a need to venture into the wilderness and seek closeness to the eternal.

On this particular night, Jacob came to a small rise and saw a light begin to arch down from the sky, a light he had not seen for twenty years. Jacob watched as angels descended the brilliant shaft. They came to him in silence and tended the pain in his soul as a doctor dresses a wound. Jacob felt like air, like a spiral of smoke ascending from a fire—visible, yet without substance. Angels reached around and through him until he was one with them. Without a word, they directed him to lie down. His fatigue was great, and he soon fell asleep.

It was still dark when Jacob awoke. A lightness of being lifted his feet over the rocks on the way back to his tent. A sense of calm had come into him that he had never known. "I will call this place 'Mahanaim,'" he thought, "'camp,' for this is truly a camp of the angels."

The next morning when they continued their journey toward Canaan, Jacob was in a state removed. Each thought was clear as the water of a well. Everything he did was effortless. He could hear the voices of his wives and children, and he answered to them, but the larger part of his being was still buoyed by the angelic luminosity of his soul.

Soon they were wading through shallow water at the ford of River Jabbok. Jacob and his servants helped the entire family to cross the river—his wives and slave wives and his eleven children. Rachel and Joseph—Jacob's youngest son and the only one born to his true love—were the last to cross.

"Joseph," Jacob said, as he waded next to the camel and steadied the boy on the litter, "the water would be over your head. Look, it is above the camel's knees."

"No father, it is not over my head. Can't you see? My head is higher than yours!"

Jacob caught Rachel's eye, and she shrugged, "See, he is just like his father."

Night had fallen by the time every person and all the animals had crossed safely. While the evening meal was being served, something called Jacob back across the river. It was not a voice but a tugging at his spirit. When he waded up out of the water and onto the far bank, he found a stranger standing there—a tall and powerfully muscled individual clothed in flowing white robes.

"Who are you?" asked Jacob. But the stranger did not answer.

"Need I ask again?" demanded Jacob. "Who are you?"

Silence.

Possessed by a fear that this mute interloper might cross the river and harm his family, Jacob seized him and, with a mighty effort, threw him to the ground. All through the night Jacob wrestled with the stranger. Feeling Jacob's surprising strength, the stranger struck a fearsome blow and dislocated Jacob's hip. Stars made their nightly turn, the moon rose and fell near to the horizon, but still Jacob and the stranger held on.

When the sky began to blush, the stranger spoke for the first time. "Release me. Daybreak is upon us!"

"Not until you bless me!" Jacob demanded.

"What do they call you?"

"Jacob."

"Your name is now Israel, for you have proven your strength against the Almighty."

"Who are you?" asked Jacob once more.

"What is it to you? Is it not enough that you have witnessed the force of God? Your strength of spirit is great. From this day forth, you will conquer your foes, however mighty they may be. Here is my blessing!"

Then the stranger rose to a great height and towered over Jacob. He unfurled his white robes until they shimmered. At that instant, the first rays of sunlight broke over the horizon directly behind the stranger. Jacob held up both hands to shield his eyes from the blinding glare. When he was able to see again, the stranger was gone.

Jacob fell to his knees out of fear and exhaustion. Raising his hands heavenward, he said, "Here, on this Earth, I have seen the face of God. This place shall be known as Peniel."

Struggling to his feet, Jacob turned his back on the rising sun and limped across to the other shore, where his family was awakening to a new day.

He struggled over toward Rachel's tent to tell her what had happened. Stepping into the dim light, he heard the faint sounds of suckling. The air smelled faintly sweet and musty, as of milk and wet fur.

"Father!" said Joseph. "She-wolf has had babies!"

Jacob groaned as he bent down to rub the boy's head. Then he picked up one of the newborn pups and held it out for Rachel to see.

"Oh, yes, Husband," she said. "Joseph has made sure that I've had a good, close look at every single one. They're very sweet."

"Sweet?" said Jacob. "Perhaps, but also hungry! How will we feed them all after they are weaned?"

"We'll feed them some of the meat from the extra flock of sheep we'll be able to keep because they're so well protected by She-dog's offspring."

"Well put," said Jacob, as the pup licked him on the mouth.

"Jacob, why are you limping? And what has soiled your clothes?"

"Once we're on our way, I'll ride with you for a time and tell you what happened last night. But I will say this—it was a sign that things will go well for us."

## — 10 —

Jacob knew that they had entered the land of his kinsmen and were nearing the River Jordan. He was also aware that if Esau should discover their presence before Jacob announced that they were coming, it would not portend well for their arrival. Before they left the encampment that morning, he sent a group of messengers out ahead to find Esau and speak with him.

"Tell my brother that I have returned from the house of Laban. I am coming home with my wives and children, my servants and slaves, my flocks and herds. Say that we come bearing gifts and with goodwill."

Later that day, the messengers returned. "Master, your brother is on the move with four hundred men. We should meet up with them by evening. What should we do?"

"First, we are going to split up. You," said Jacob to one of his most trusted servants, "take all the women and children and remain behind, well hidden in the hills. If things go well, we will return for you."

"For the rest of you, this is how it will go: Divide the sheep, goats, and camels into droves, each with two hundred females and twenty males. Pull together a final drove of cows and bulls, asses and donkeys. Drive the sheep toward Esau, then the goats, the camels, and the other animals. Leave with about an hour in between each drove. When each of you reaches Esau, tell him that the animals are a gift from his brother, Jacob, who is following.

Throughout that day, as Esau and his men made their way north toward Jacob, they met with a wave of droves in their path, accompanied by clouds of dust, a cacophony of noise, and abundant droppings. The greetings with each round of Jacob's servants, and the sudden arrival of large groups of animals to care for, slowed them down so that they had to pitch camp for another night.

The next morning, Esau and his men finally met up with Jacob. Esau walked toward his brother, and Jacob bowed out of respect. Jacob's loose, flowing robes were those of a shepherd. Esau's garb and hardened demeanor were those of a warrior, the leather creaking as he moved.

Without a greeting, Esau suddenly brandished his sword, saying, "So, Jacob, I see that nothing has changed. You sent others ahead to wage your battle. We had to fight through your advance forces before we could finally get to *you*. The army of sheep wasn't too much of a challenge, but the goats did have those nasty horns. And the camels … well … what with all the belching and sour breath … we barely survived them!"

"But Brother, Esau, I was not trying to …"

"Jacob, Jacob, I jest!" said Esau as he smoothly sheathed his sword.

With that, Esau rushed up to Jacob and embraced him open armed. Jacob could now see that his brother was indeed glad to see him. When they both separated and looked at each other, the eyes that had not met for more than twenty years were clouded with tears.

"Esau," said Jacob at last. "It truly is good to lay eyes on you again, now that I know you are not still angry with me."

"Jacob, we were both children then. But tell me, where is your family?"

"They are safe in the hills." With that, Jacob turned and motioned to one of his servants, who mounted a camel and went off to summon Rachel, Leah, and the others.

"Safe from whom? Me? Brother, I can see that your imagination has suffered nothing over the years."

"Come," said Jacob. "Walk with me. There is much to tell."

As they walked and waited for Jacob's family to arrive, Jacob and Esau shared the stories of their lives during the last twenty years. To his surprise, Esau could see that Jacob, who was such a mother's boy as a child, had grown knowledgeable about the land and become an accomplished herdsman. Likewise, Jacob listened with interest as Esau, who once embodied the independent spirit of the wilderness, expressed a deep love for his family and extolled the joys of spending time at home with his wives and children. Even though they had been apart for so many years, they now discovered that the centers of their lives had grown closer.

When a messenger came to tell them that Jacob's family had returned, they made their way back to the meeting point. She-wolf ran up to Jacob with tail wagging, then turned on Esau and sent him reeling.

"Brother," teased Jacob, "don't tell me that you are afraid of my little dog here. She is as tame as a kitten."

"Leave it to you, Jacob, to take a fierce animal and turn it into a servant and a nursemaid!"

"Things are not always as they seem, Brother," said Jacob.

"This is true," Esau agreed, "and people can have a change of heart."

"Well said. And age begets wisdom?" continued Jacob, reaching.

"On that count," Esau observed, "it depends on who is aging."

It took some time to reorganize for the journey to Canaan. When everything was finally ready, Jacob and Esau led the contingent. They were followed by Rachel, Leah, and the children, along with Bilhah and Zilpah. The servants and other slaves came next, in front of the great flocks of sheep and herds of camels and goats, then oxen, ass, and donkeys. On either side of this expansive array of people and animals were stationed two hundred soldiers who answered to Esau.

As the procession cut an impressive swath through the country-side, Esau gave Jacob the news of his parents, Isaac and Rebekah. He told him of his own wives from the land of Canaan, and of the scores of heirs they had given him over the last twenty years. Jacob described his life in the house of Laban, recounting the joys and satisfactions, the duplicities and deceptions. Jacob was relieved of a great burden as he told his story to Esau, for he had not been able to share it with anyone in the close-knit city of Paddan-aram, lest his words find the ears of Laban.

Denizens of that wide-open region could see the dust coming from miles away. As the phalanx approached, they could hear the camels' hooves—a harbinger of the snorts, grunts, and smells that were to accompany the horde. People came out to greet them as they passed through open spaces where shepherds tended their flocks and skirted the edges of encampments and cities. No one could remember seeing such a magnificent, orderly assemblage of life moving with such efficiency and purpose, other than the seasonal migrations of geese overhead.

By nightfall they entered a forest that fringed the banks of a small river. From the lithe limbs of willow they made small houses for themselves and lean-tos to protect the animals for the night. They named that place Succoth, "a shelter made of branches."

That evening along the riverbank, Rachel and Jacob sat beneath the sheltering leaves. With the children well cared for and Esau's forces encamped nearby, they felt free and safe for the first time in as long as they could remember. Listening to the soft voice of the water and the fluttering leaves, and brushed by the cool night air, Jacob was enveloped in the tincture that he had come to know as the scent of his true love. He ran his fingers through her thick hair. An owl called. Something skittered past in the underbrush. But the world around them vanished.

Flowers.

Cinnamon.

## — 11 —

As Jacob slept that night, God appeared to him and said, "Prepare your people and lead them into the land of beth El. There they will worship the one God."

At daybreak, Esau came to Jacob. "I must gather my own house and begin the journey to Seir."

"Why must you go? Are we never to share the same land?"

"Jacob, our lineage is blessed with more heirs and descendants than we can name, but this land is not big enough to support them all, especially with our vast flocks and herds of animals. My people will move on to the land of Seir. It is a beautiful place of mountains and valleys where we can live well."

Parting after such a brief time together pained the two brothers deeply. They embraced for a long time before separating.

"Esau," said Jacob at last, "it has brought me great joy to be reconciled with you. I am grateful for your help on this part of my journey."

Esau said nothing. He simply bowed deeply to Jacob, then to Jacob's family, mounted his camel, motioned for his soldiers to follow, and was lost in the dust and thunder of hooves.

Jacob gathered all his wives and servants under the branches of a great oak tree. "We are going to begin the last part of our pilgrimage to beth El, the place where I was visited by Yahweh. Go back to your tents and gather any jewelry, statues, or other possessions that serve as idols to other gods. Bring them here."

While everyone returned to their tents to do as Jacob asked, he dug a large hole near the roots of the oak. "Come, place them inside," said Jacob to each person that returned with the idols.

Rachel was the last to approach the hole. Jacob gestured for her to place her things there along with the others. She held a large satchel, and Jacob could tell by how she cradled the bag that the contents meant much to her. For a long moment she stood at the edge of the hole, unable to let go of her belongings. Again, Jacob silently gestured. After hesitating once more, then looking up at Jacob and seeing his resolve, she gently added her belongings to the others. Immediately, Jacob covered the idols with a deep layer of earth. Servants helped him to roll several large stones over that place so that it would never again be disturbed.

Rachel wept.

At last, they crossed the River Jordan and traveled west into the hill country. Then they turned south toward beth El and Mamre beyond. It was a beautiful land with large swaths of forest that were riven with streams and ribboned with swards of meadow. Stately cedars of Lebanon grew on the cooler rises, the smell of incense wafting up as needles were crushed underfoot. Oaks adorned the windward slopes. Arching branches of willow graced the edges of streams. Some valleys were planted with groves of olive trees, pistachios, and almonds. Fields shimmered with the blossoms of fitches, a kind of wild pea, and patches of crimson lilies. Every so often they passed through a wild garden pregnant with the intoxicating scent of the five-petaled flowers of mandrake. Butterflies flitted on their ceaseless hunt for nectar.

Passing beneath the sun-speckled shade in a grove of magnificent oaks, many of Jacob's sons were walking with him as he answered questions about the plants and animals that they saw and heard. Young Joseph was riding on his father's shoulders.

Little Zebulun was holding Jacob's hand. "Father, can I ride on your shoulders now? Please?"

"Be patient son. You will have your turn in a little while."

A cuckoo began to call, and Joseph asked, "Father, what is that?"

The other children also bent their ears to the answer. "That is the sound of the cuckoo. It is a strange bird that does not make a nest of its own."

"So where does it nest, then?" asked Jacob's eldest son, Reuben.

"It lays its eggs in the nests of other smaller birds. Then, when the young cuckoo chicks hatch and grow, they knock the smaller chicks out of the nest and eat the food gathered by the parents of the other birds."

"It doesn't sound like a very nice bird!" said Joseph.

"Nature has its own ways," Jacob replied, "a code that is different from ours. Yahweh tells us to share what we have and to take care of those who are less fortunate."

"But I have seen a cuckoo, and it is a beautiful bird," said Levi, one of the older boys.

"Its song is very loud," added Zebulun.

"And it keeps going on and on, like our sister Dinah," said Simeon.

"How do you mean?" asked Jacob.

To which Simeon replied, "Once she starts talking, she never stops!"

Everyone laughed, and even Jacob smiled. Then he said, "Sons, be kind to your sister. There are eleven of you, but only one Dinah. It's your job to be nice and make sure that no harm comes to her."

After a few days' travel they reached the site of beth El. That night as they sat around the fire, Jacob told his family about his flight from Mamre and how he spent a night where they were now camping. The next morning, Jacob instructed each of his children to bring a stone to the small altar that he had erected on that site twenty years ago. Jacob used the stones to enlarge the altar. He put the bigger stones on the bottom and feathered them together, then tapered the mound up with the smaller stones on top. Once the altar was finished, Jacob anointed it with oil that had been infused with the scent of myrrh.

Three days later, Jacob's family and their entourage arrived at Mamre in Hebron, the place also known as Kiriath-arba. They pitched their tents on the outskirts of the city, then Jacob, Leah, and Rachel walked to the house of Jacob's family. When the servants ushered them into the house, they found Rebekah, a very old woman whose back was deeply stooped, tending to Isaac, who was blind and gravely ill.

Jacob entered Isaac's bedroom, and Rebekah squinted to see who it was, for her own eyesight was not good. The air was stale. It smelled of incense and unguents.

"Mother, it is me—your son, Jacob."

"Jacob?" she said feebly. "Is that you, Son?"

Jacob went over to embrace his mother as tears ran from her clouded eyes.

Then Jacob bent over his father's bed and said aloud, "Hello, Father."

Isaac's head turned, but his eyes remained fixed straight ahead and focused as if looking off to a great distance.

"Jacob? I thought I heard Rebekah say your name. It is good to hear your voice, Son. Come here," said Isaac, and the two embraced.

"Where are your wives?"

"I'll get them this instant, Father."

Jacob went back outside and asked Rachel and Leah to join him.

"Come close so I can see you," said Isaac.

First Rachel, and then Leah, bent down so Isaac could touch their faces.

"You are both so beautiful," said Isaac. "Jacob is blessed. And children? When will I meet my grandchildren? Don't keep an old man waiting!"

Rachel and Leah went to get the children while Jacob sat and listened as Rebekah began to tell him what he had missed during the many years since he had fled northward to live in the house of her brother Laban.

When the children arrived, they all crowded into Isaac's bedroom and stood in a circle around his bed. Jacob helped Rebekah to make her way through the crowd and sit on the bed next to Isaac.

"All of you," said Isaac, "welcome to the house of your grandfather Isaac and grandmother Rebekah. We are happy to have you visit.

Now I want each one of you to say your name and tell us your age so we can hear your voices."

Rebekah looked on, and Isaac nodded his head as each child spoke in turn. After all eleven boys had introduced themselves, Dinah finally said, "Hello Grandmother and Grandfather, it is me, Dinah."

At that moment, Rebekah raised her hands as if in prayer and said, "Praise Yahweh, there is a girl!" Everyone laughed as Dinah's face turned the color of new wine.

Once the introductions were over, the servants prepared a feast that seemed like it could feed a multitude but was barely enough. As Jacob and his wives and eldest children sat nearby, Rebekah continued the story of her life with Isaac.

That night, after the children had gone off to their tents to sleep, Jacob and his wives spoke with Rebekah.

"How long does he have?" asked Leah.

"I don't know, dear," answered Rebekah. "Perhaps a few days, not more."

"How old is he now?" Rachel asked.

"He has lived for one hundred and eighty years," she said. "He is now five years older than the age when his father, Abraham, died."

At daybreak Jacob sent his two fleetest messengers to Seir to tell Esau that Isaac was on his deathbed and that he should come at once. When it did not look like her husband would last the week that it would take for word to reach Esau and for him to return, Rebekah told Isaac that Esau was coming. This had the desired effect, and Isaac rallied for one last time.

Within hours of Esau's arrival, Isaac was free of this world. As his spirit began to rise, Isaac looked back. Freed of the blindness that had burdened him for over twenty years, he could finally see the faces of his entire family. In the beauty of their expressions—even when caught in that moment of grief—Isaac knew that he at last beheld the face of God.

At sunrise the next day, with all his family gathered, Isaac was placed near his mother and father, Abraham and Sarah, in the tomb at Machpelah near Mamre.

When Esau entered the tomb, he knelt down and said, "Father, I will always be grateful for how you taught me to love and understand the wonders of creation." He gently lifted Isaac's hands and placed under them several ancient, faded feathers from an eagle's wing, feathers that once cut the air during a legendary battle in the skies.

"I return this gift to you, Father. May the feathers of your beloved eagle carry you swiftly to the gate of heaven."

# — 12 —

Following the burial, Jacob and his family decided to remain in Mamre for the rest of the growing season to help Rebekah manage the harvest.

One evening, after they had lived in Mamre for a time, Rachel came to Jacob and said, "Come walk with me."

She took his hand and led him out into some of the vineyards just beyond the edge of the city.

"Here," she said, holding a plump, sweet grape up to his mouth.

When he opened his mouth to respond, she stuffed the grape inside.

"That was delicious!" he said.

"How many grapes does it take to make a cluster?" she asked.

"What are you talking about?"

Now she held up a perfectly shaped cluster that ended with a single grape at the tip.

"See this grape?"

"Of course I do," said Jacob, even more puzzled.

"This is the grape that we created on the riverbank that night two moons ago."

Looking into his eyes, Rachel could see that he was beginning to understand her meaning. Jacob threw his arms around her and said, "How I do love you! We have been so blessed!"

In a whirlwind of heat and work, punctuated by periods of play and more than a few squabbles, the summer flew by and the season of harvesting arrived. Everyone worked long and hard to cut the wheat and barley and thresh the grains. As each crop ripened in turn, even the younger children helped to gather the soft figs and sugary grapes, to pick the olives, almonds, and walnuts. They especially enjoyed plucking and cleaning the sticky dates, although a few of the youngest got sick by eating far too many of the plump, irresistible delicacies.

One day out in the vineyard, Jacob picked the biggest grape he could find and brought it to Rachel, who was reclining in the shade and was heavy with child.

Jacob sat down beside her and held out the grape. "Looking at you now, wife, I would have to agree with what you said some months ago."

"And what was that?" she said, tilting her head and eyeing him with suspicion.

Holding the purple fruit in front of her abdomen, he said, "You must, indeed, be carrying a very large grape."

"Can I have that one?" she asked, putting her hand out.

As soon as he gave it to her, she squished it on his face and rubbed it in, hard, laughing as she did. "Think about that the next time you have the urge to plant another *grape* in my vineyard!"

Some weeks later, when the harvest had been brought in and the work was done, everyone said their goodbyes to Rebekah, and the entire house of Jacob followed the trail north, back toward beth El.

One night, a few days into the journey, Rachel shook Jacob awake and said, "Quickly, go and get the midwife. My water has come and I am going into labor."

Jacob summoned the midwife at once, and she began to prepare for the birth. Within an hour, Rachel's labor quickly transformed from severe discomfort into excruciating pain.

"Do something, please!" she screamed. "My insides are tearing apart."

"The child is coming very quickly, dear," said the midwife. "It won't be much longer. Keep pushing. Breathe. Now push again. Yes, here we are. I can see the head now."

With one final effort that consumed everything Rachel had to give, the baby emerged. Its cries immediately filled the tent.

"Another boy!" announced the midwife.

But Rachel did not answer. Something had riven inside of her, a tear from which her blood and spirit were freely flowing. Using her last vestige of energy, she reached up and pulled Jacob's head down.

"Jacob," she whispered.

He placed his hand behind her head and moved his ear next to her mouth.

With her last words, Rachel breathed, "Ben-oni."

Then, her head lolled back, and Jacob could feel its full weight upon his hand. He watched, helpless, as her life force became a river of red, streaming over the bedclothes and soaking into the desert sand. Flowing, ferric, and final.

"Leave me alone with her," Jacob ordered the midwife.

"But the child," she said, holding out his son.

"Leave me!"

When he was alone, Jacob sat and stroked Rachel's hair. He kissed her forehead and, softly, her lips. Then he gently breathed into her open mouth and said, "Ben-oni.

"Here, my love, take something of my life with you. I will see you again, as I have seen the face of God."

Jacob knew that he would never again hear her gentle voice or feel the sweet touch that sent a pulse of excitement through his being as none other could. In that instant, his own world was rent, like a great tapestry torn apart. Where once there had been an enfolding life with his true love, now there was a hole in his heart that seemed big enough to swallow his joy, but far too small to encompass his grief.

All that night, Jacob kept vigil at his beloved's side. The next morning when he emerged from the tent, the midwife came to him holding his new son. Jacob took the child into his arms and cradled him there.

"Hello little one," he said. "It's your father, Jacob. What a beautiful child," he said looking up at the midwife. "His eyes are so full of life. Rachel's life."

She nodded in silence.

"You will not be called Ben-oni, 'son of my sorrow,'" said Jacob. "I will call you Benjamin, 'son of a good omen,' the second son of my beloved."

All that day, as the nurse and midwife prepared Rachel for burial, Jacob and some of his strongest servants dug the grave on a small rise not far from where she had died. Then they used a camel and a litter to drag a tall, thin stone to that place.

Rachel was buried, as the sun was setting, along the road to Ephrath in a land that was known as Bethlehem. Using ropes and stakes, the natural obelisk they had brought to that place was raised as a monument. It was erected so that the setting harvest sun kissed the top of the stone and cast a shadow that pointed to the very place where the light in Rachel's eyes had flickered its last.

# — 13 —

After leaving that place and traveling for two more days, Jacob and his family reached beth El—the region where they would settle for many years. Once the tents had been erected and the meal was being served, Jacob stole away into the night.

First, he went into his own tent and found a parcel of ancient camel skin, which he slipped into his satchel. Then he went to the flock and picked out the finest lamb he could find. Carrying the lamb, he walked for some time until he reached the altar at beth El where he had been visited by Yahweh and the angels when he was a young man fleeing across the desert to escape the wrath of Esau.

Jacob placed the lamb atop the altar and began to pray. His words to Yahweh were soft and swift, as supple as the wind that blows through the waves of harvest wheat. When he had finished praying, Jacob unwrapped the knife that his mother had given him the night he had first fled from home. He slipped off the ivory scabbard, gripped the ram's-horn handle, and deftly drew the sharp edge across the lamb's throat. As its blood flowed onto the capstone of the altar, then down the sides of the cairn, Jacob once again saw the lifeblood draining from his beloved Rachel, and he fell to his knees, overcome with despair and grief as black as a starless night.

Then, before his eyes, the fleece of the lamb began to spark and glow. Suddenly, it burst into streamers of light with an explosion that boomed and drove Jacob down onto his back. As he lay prostrate beneath the desert night, he saw a fountain of light reach heavenward, expanding out from the altar until the brilliant rays touched every part of the sky. Jacob saw that each point of light burned into the fabric of the heavens to form a new star.

Yahweh called out in a voice that rolled like thunder, "Jacob, I hear your prayers. Your grief will be transformed into hope. Isaac lives on in you and in every branch of your family's great tree. Rachel waits for you, here, at my side, and for all time.

"You have kept faith and honored our covenant. Long after you are gone, your descendants will number as the stars. Have faith, Jacob. I will not forsake you."

# JOSEPH

*"I have heard it said that you can understand and interpret dreams."*

*"Not I, but God."*

Genesis 41:15

# — 1 —

Joseph awoke drenched in sweat, caught in a confusing maelstrom, hovering on dreamers's wings somewhere between dread and elation. His last vision shone with a sense of clarity and purpose. But what could it mean?

The dream had begun under a blue sky during the harvest. The fields were alive, a whispering sea of grain being cut and bundled. At high sun, everyone sat in the shade of a large cedar and ate a midday meal: thankful for the rest, remarking on the quality and abundance of this season's wheat.

When all had returned to work, Joseph walked into the center of the field where there stood a large sheaf of wheat. As he stopped to stare at the mass of carefully laid stalks, his perspective changed. Now *he* was the sheaf of grain, which stood on end and towered above the field. From that height Joseph could see his brothers arrayed in the distance. Each of them had cut a large mound of grain. They turned and noticed him in their midst. All at once his brothers were transformed into sheaves, gliding closer, then encircling him and bowing low.

Joseph told no one. He knew his brothers strongly resented how their father favored him—firstborn son to Rachel. Jacob sheltered Joseph from the verbal jibes and occasional physical blows from his siblings, which made them even more jealous.

"What's the matter, Joseph? Can't you take care of yourself? Are you afraid of your own brothers?"

Some said that Joseph was his father's favorite son because he was the tallest and most handsome of his brothers. Others disagreed, "No, it is because he reminds him of Rachel."

In Joseph, Jacob still saw the bright-eyed child riding on his shoulders. But to others, Joseph was too earnest, too self-assured—and with good reason. He had always received what he asked for, to the point where others detected an air of entitlement. Joseph felt things deeply and loved even those who could not love him. He was a walking contradiction of strength and sentimentality.

Even his coat had become a source of derision. A gift from his father, who had it made from the softest, lightest lamb's wool, it fit him perfectly and reached down nearly to the ground. The coat exaggerated his height and caused him to seem even taller. One more thing to mock.

All of them were unaware of the one thing that really set Joseph apart. It was a force that could cast a shadow over the light of his own consciousness—a gift of prophecy that was always poised, ready to strike and rattle his world. His dreams came unbidden—as jarring and undeniable as the call of a horned owl in the night.

In his next vision, Joseph saw himself as a star in the center of the sky. He marveled at how the vast, cold space somehow held him fast. Then his father, mother, and brothers began walking toward him. They started to dance, raising sparkles of light with their feet, light that arced around them and transformed their very beings into the sun, moon, and stars. Faster and faster they moved until blurring to form a ring of rippling light that revolved around Joseph.

He awoke with a start—cold, dizzy, and imbued with a sense of his own power. This time, driven by a need to understand, Joseph ignored his better instincts and shared this dream with his father and brothers. But even he could not have suspected how a mere dream could split the fabric of his family.

# — 2 —

Joseph's father, Jacob, now used the name Israel that Yahweh had bestowed upon him at Peniel. Israel was well advanced in years and was not able to travel very far or easily.

One day Israel said, "Son, go out to the pastures and join your brothers where they are tending the sheep. Come back by nightfall and bring me news of the flock."

"Where are they, Father?"

"I believe they are in the pastures at Shechem."

As he began the journey, Joseph was glad that he had a younger brother, Benjamin, otherwise he would never be allowed to travel. Their father would not let them both out of his sight at the same time.

Along the road in Shechem, Joseph met a passerby who told him the flocks had moved on to the neighboring region of Dothan. He continued in that direction, walking through some of the most beautiful land in that region. The River Jordan flowed through the lowlands to the east and from there the land rose up and folded into hills and valleys that harbored remote streams and forests. The scent of cedar in the uplands, the timeless groves of majestic oaks along the slopes, the verge of broad intervening meadows, and the supple greens of willows binding the streambanks—these were the living marks of Joseph's homeland. He heard a lanner falcon cry out and caught a fleeting glimpse as it disappeared behind a rise to the west. Beyond, where Joseph scanned a further range, his eyes caught the distant azure of the Great Sea stretching away to a nebulous gray horizon.

But dark clouds mustered beyond the hollows of those distant hills. Deep and thick does the river of hatred flow when fed by the springs of jealousy. Joseph's older brothers whiled far too much time in the fields and had not enough work. Israel's sons by Leah, especially Levi and Zebulun, were strong in their conviction that something must be done to punish Joseph for his perceived slights and to avenge the many gifts and privileges he received from Israel, which they felt should have been bestowed on them.

Several hours before sunset, Levi said to his brothers, "It's getting late in the day. Joseph should be coming along soon, as he always does, to spy on us for Father."

"Why don't we just run him through with our swords?" joked Zebulun.

"We can tell Father that he was impaled by a goat in rut!" said Issachar, to a round of laughter.

"You have the wits of a coney," Naphtali spat with his familiar barbed tongue.

"You have the guile of a jackal," Issachar retorted.

"Mutton brain."

"Donkey pie!"

"Camel's breath."

As this string of insults continued, they grew more detailed and gained a note of serious intent.

"Why waste our breath insulting each other?" asked Naphtali. "We taunt Joseph now because he is Father's favorite. But what will happen later when it comes time to dole out the inheritance? Where will we be then—begging Joseph for a few crumbs? Better to get rid of him while we can."

At that moment, Joseph arrived in their midst. Levi and Simeon grabbed and held Joseph, while Judah and Zebulun stripped off his coat. Then the others began to beat him.

"What are you doing?" Joseph demanded, as he spat blood that oozed from a cut lip. "I did nothing to offend you."

"You *are* the offense!" Levi asserted.

"Stop!" said Reuben, who was the oldest among them. "We are not going to kill our own brother. Are we no better than a pack of jackals?"

"It's time for action!" argued Judah.

Trying to avoid further bloodshed, Reuben quickly offered another plan.

"I like that idea," said Judah. "Here, Brother, dream your way out of this!" Judah mocked.

At that, four of the brothers each took one of Joseph's arms or legs and carried him, struggling, over to a nearby well, which was dry. They flung him into the well, where he landed with a thud and a groan. He lay there, unconscious.

"Now settle down and get back to work!" ordered Reuben. "I've got to tend to the flock in the farthest pasture. When I return, we can pull Joseph out of the well and bring him home."

After Reuben had been gone for some time, Dan looked up and said, "Someone's coming! What are we going to do now?"

A group of Ishmaelite merchants were walking their camels up the road that led past the well. They were traveling from Gilead with herbs, incense, spices, and gum to trade for other valuables in Egypt.

"May we draw some water from this well?" one of the travelers asked.

"If it had water to draw, you would be welcome," answered Zebulun.

"What?" remarked one of the strangers as he peered into the hole. "There is a half-naked man in this dust bowl."

"Yes, it is some slave that we found who had fallen in," said Simeon. "But he said that if we agreed to pull him out, he would pledge himself to our service."

"He looks to be lean and strong," said one of the Ishmaelites.

Thinking quickly, Simeon said, "Would you like to buy him?"

"How much?"

"Twenty pieces of silver."

Down in the well, Joseph had been lying unconscious for some time. In this state, he was vaguely aware of being surrounded by the smell of hot dirt, as if he had been swallowed into an arid nether-world. He was just beginning to stir, when the merchants tried to pull him from the well. As he resisted and clutched at the powdery dirt, his hand closed around something hard and round, flat on one side and extremely heavy for its size. Mustering his wits, he quickly hid it in an inner pocket of his tunic.

Joseph's brothers watched as his hands were bound by the strangers. He endured the treatment silently, knowing that he could not possibly overpower so many men. "God will protect me," he thought.

As he was led away, he looked back at his brothers with an expression of pity and remorse, rather than the spit and anger that would have given them something to bite into, to *love,* even. How could they embrace this enigma named Joseph? To their eyes, his resignation was a final act of condescension, which caused their hostility to flare even brighter and fueled it into a recklessness.

And they were right, he could not be touched, for nothing compared to the pain he always carried within him of his mother's death, which he pulled around his heart like the smooth, ashen bark of an olive tree.

When Reuben returned from his work in the far pasture, he said, "Brothers, how fares Joseph?" Leaning over the well, he saw that it was empty. Reuben grabbed Zebulun by the front of his robes and screamed, "Brother, where is Joseph?"

"We sold him to a passing band of merchants for twenty pieces of silver."

"Where are they taking him?"

"To sell him for a slave in Egypt."

In a fit of rage, Reuben tore the front of his shirt open and bellowed, "Fools! What have you done? This will turn Israel against all of us! We must get Joseph back."

"They easily outnumber us and are well armed," said Levi.

"Where are the pieces of silver?" demanded Reuben as he held out his open hand. "Give them to me."

Zebulun handed him the pouch of coins.

"This is what you have just done to your future and to your own flesh and blood!" Reuben screamed as he took the pieces of silver and flung them far out into the pasture, where the coins scattered and became lost in the deep grass. "This news will break Father's heart."

Late that night, when Joseph's brothers returned home, Israel asked, "Where is Joseph? I sent him off to help you with the flock."

Simeon solemnly held out Joseph's coat, which they had soaked with the blood of a goat. "This is all we found," he said. "Our brother was attacked and killed by a pack of jackals."

Israel took the coat into his hands, then stared at the bloodstains—frozen into a stunned, uncomprehending silence.

"Father?"

"You must be mistaken," Israel insisted with a quavering voice. "I just saw him this morning!"

Then Israel looked up and read the faces of his sons. His hands tightened around the remnants of Joseph's coat. As his brief wall of denial began to crumble, he was wracked with paroxysms of grief.

"No, *no!*" Israel screamed as he pulled at his hair and tore his clothes. "Not my boy Joseph. Yahweh, no!"

Israel held the coat up to his face. His tears dripped onto the garment and ran red with the smears of blood.

After some time had passed, Israel lowered the garment and addressed his sons in a scathing tone—with a vehemence that startled them.

"Did you search for him?" he demanded.

"This is all that we could find."

"Are you absolutely certain?"

"Father, he is gone."

"Go search again! And don't return until you find him!"

In a daze, Israel wandered off into the night, lost in grief. After walking for a time, he stopped and leaned against a rock. "Rachel, please forgive me," he lamented. "I should have kept him closer, watched over him more carefully. Every time I looked at him, I saw you in his eyes. How will I live without both of you?"

He lowered his head. Tears fell and washed the dust from the stone.

"Why, Yahweh?" he lamented. "After I have prayed and kept my faith for all these long years. Why?"

## — 3 —

The Ishmaelite merchants bound Joseph's wrists and forced him to walk the long road to Egypt while tethered to the back of a camel. After two days of traveling together toward the south and west, the merchants discovered that Joseph was no brute, but a bright, likeable young man. When he assured them that he would not flee, they untied his wrists.

Their long, arduous journey skirted the Wilderness of Shur, passed south of the Bitter Lakes, and continued toward the River Nile. As the caravan at last neared their destination for trade along the great river, a magnificent pyramid loomed before them. Awestruck, Joseph asked his captors, "What is that?"

"That is the great pyramid of Khufu," answered one. "I am told that its tip rises nearly three hundred cubits into the sky."

They rounded the base of the great pyramid, only to see another, smaller one that had been hidden behind it, and another that was still smaller in the distance.

"And those?" asked Joseph.

"The next is the pyramid of Khafre, and the third one is that of Menkaure."

"I have heard tell of these pyramids," said Joseph. "I could never have imagined their grandeur. The people who built them must have had very strong faith."

"The people who built them were slaves who were forced to live and die moving great blocks of stone that each weighed as much as four camels."

"And what is that stone beast?" asked Joseph.

"That is the sphinx. Another one of Khafre's monuments to himself—half human and half lion."

"And half brain, I hear," said another of the Ishmaelites. "The 'great kings' of Egypt are so inbred, I hear they father their own siblings."

After several days of trading wares in the shadows of the pyramids, the merchants were not pleased with the offers they had received for Joseph. Following a long and, at times, heated discussion, they decided who they thought would pay the greatest sum for their young, intelligent captive. They took Joseph to the home of Potiphar, commander of the guards of Pharaoh Apophis.

"We have a slave for sale," they said to Potiphar. "He is young, strong, and intelligent."

"How old are you?" asked Potiphar, seeing not only an able-bodied slave but the possibility to mold the mind of a youth.

"Seventeen years," replied Joseph.

That night—his first as Potiphar's new slave—Joseph lay on a bedroll in a small, cramped room. He held the object that was buried at the bottom of the well and looked at it closely. It was a small, one-sided sculpture, a sort of medallion painstakingly fashioned into the shape of a large silver beetle. Its shell was ringed with six rubies, and the center of its back was inlaid with a seventh stone—a large diamond that sparkled in the moonlight. "This object must be worth a fortune," he thought. "I cannot allow anyone to find it."

Potiphar saw that Joseph was a young man of integrity, honesty, and wit. The blessing of Yahweh that lay upon Joseph's people soon brought good fortune to Potiphar's house. Joseph earned his master's confidence and was soon placed in charge of many of his affairs.

As commander of Pharaoh's army, Potiphar was often away for long periods. At these times, Potiphar's wife, who was also young, started to follow Joseph around and insinuate herself.

One day, she called to him, "Oh, Joseph, would you please come and get this water jug down? It is too high up on the shelf, and you are much taller than me." She stood close to him as he stretched to get the jug, then reached out and touched him, saying, "Let me steady you so you don't fall."

"Don't you find me attractive?" she asked.

"That is not the point," Joseph replied. "Potiphar has treated me well. I am not going to betray his trust. And what you're asking is a sin."

As Joseph handed her the vessel, she held on to his wrist, far too long for propriety. Pulling away, he said "I've had enough of this."

Angry, she grabbed hold of his tunic and tore it off as he walked away. Joseph stormed out of the house, and then she screamed, "He has forced himself on me!" All the servants heard this.

When Potiphar came home that night, she showed him the tunic and accused Joseph of seducing her. "Look, he even left his clothes behind."

Livid, Potiphar went to Joseph's room. "Is this how you honor my trust, by seducing my wife—after all I have done for you?!"

As commander of Pharaoh's army, Potiphar had his own system of justice. He had Joseph thrown into prison—a round, imposing, windowless tower of stone.

Even in that dark, dank place, Joseph did not despair. Perhaps it was his own inherent nature to remain calm and centered or the result of growing up as the favorite son, knowing that his needs would always be met. He simply knelt and prayed.

"Joseph, you have honored me this day," answered Yahweh. "Fear not, for you are in my favor and my blessing is with you."

# — 4 —

His life in the brooding prison tower brought hard work, little food, and long hours in a cramped cell. But Joseph drew upon his inner strength and good humor. It was that quality of his character that all but his jealous brothers seemed to admire. In a short time, Joseph had befriended the guards and was even asked to join them in their quarters where they played games of chance to pass the long, dreary hours.

During one such game, after listening to Joseph describe one of his dreams and tell them its meaning, a guard turned to him and asked, "Joseph, what do you make of this strange dream of mine? I was walking through the desert when a venomous asp slithered toward me. The next thing I knew, I had become the snake, and the snake was me. An eagle cried out. We both looked up just as the eagle swooped down, pierced the snake with its claws and killed it by biting its neck."

Joseph paused for a moment, deep in thought, then said, "I only have one question, which is central to understanding the deep meaning of this dream."

"What is that?" asked the guard.

"Are you a violent man?"

"Well, I've always thought of myself as being fair and just … "

At hearing this, the rest of the guards interrupted his reply with raucous laughter and nearly fell off their chairs.

"Oh sure, that's why we call him 'The Blade,'" said one of the other guards.

"But he cuts ever so gently," added another. Again they roared.

Joseph laughed along with them. Then, when everyone had fallen silent, he said, "Your dream is warning you that if you don't control your own violent nature, it will one day come to destroy you."

"And the eagle?" asked the guard.

"Look to Yahweh," Joseph replied. "Faith, alone, will save you from yourself."

In time, Joseph was taken into their confidence and he became a well-trusted aid to the warden.


One day two strange prisoners arrived at the prison under heavy guard.

"Who are they?" asked Joseph at one of the daily gatherings of the guards.

"One is Pharaoh's baker and the other serves him his wine. They were caught in a minor theft of bread and wine, or some such."

That night the new prisoners both had disturbing dreams. When they overheard rumors of Joseph's ability for divining, they approached him.

"Is it true that you can read other men's dreams?" asked one.

"They say you can see the future."

"Whatever gifts I have, come from God," Joseph replied. "Tell me."

"I was walking in a vineyard, and I stopped to look at some blossoms on the vine. I watched, and in a few moments, the blossoms on three different boughs formed clusters of grapes that ripened and poured forth into a cup, which I gave to Pharaoh."

"You will be released in three days," said Joseph. "When you again find yourself pouring wine into Pharaoh's cup, please tell him of what I have revealed to you here today. Tell him that I was kidnapped and brought here against my will, then falsely accused of a crime I never committed."

"Here is my dream," said the baker. "I was wearing a hat made of bread into which I had baked the delicate treats that Pharaoh is most fond of."

"I am only a messenger," said Joseph, who was reluctant to reveal his reading of this dream.

"And it is only a dream," said the baker. "So tell me what it means?"

"You will also be freed in three days."

"Excellent!" said the baker, as he slapped Joseph on the back.

"But …" continued Joseph.

"What?" asked the baker.

"Pharaoh will sentence you to death to make an example for others, and three griffon vultures will pick your bones clean."

Three days went by and Joseph's foreshadowings came true. Word of his gift quickly spread among those who were close to Pharaoh. But, for Joseph, nothing changed. As the moons of two years passed and he remained a prisoner, Joseph knew that his faith was being tested.

"Yahweh, you are teaching me patience. I see that clearly. So I will be patient."

# — 5 —

At about that time, Pharaoh Apophis came to his chief sage, look-ing tired and wan.

"Highness, what has happened?"

"My dreams are tormenting me."

"Tell me," said the sage. But when Apophis had finished recalling his dreams, the sage said, "They are just dreams about sheep and wheat. Of what significance could they be?"

At wits' end, Apophis summoned Joseph to hear his dreams.

Later that same day, guards escorted Joseph from the round tower of the prison, bathed and clean-shaven. He was ushered into a lavish room.

Joseph bowed deeply to Apophis. "Highness."

"Welcome," said Apophis. "I hear that you are a man who knows dreams."

"If I may serve you in some small way, I would be honored."

"In one dream, I was standing in a field full of rounded sheep with thick wool. The Nile was in the distance, winding through its banks. Then the river became an enormous asp. When it opened its gargan-tuan mouth, a pack of seven hungry wolves came bounding forth and attacked. Seven sheep broke out from the others and were savagely torn apart until there was nothing left but bones and tufts of fur."

"Go on," said Joseph.

"I dreamed that seven rich stalks of wheat were waving in the wind. The kernels were full and ready to harvest. Then I heard a buzzing in the back of my head. This terrifying sound grew louder until a hot, dry desert wind rushed forth from my lips bearing seven great locusts. In a brief moment, the ravenous beasts devoured the wheat, then the stalks shriveled before my eyes."

Joseph was still for some time. "Highness, the meaning of your dreams is clear. The plump sheep and rich harvest of wheat are a sign that your kingdom is going to see seven years of abundance when many will prosper."

"And what of the wolves and locusts and heat?"

"Then, borne on a scorching wind from the east, will come seven years of famine. Thousands will become weak with hunger, leading to sickness, starvation, and death. The poverty of these years will be so deep that your people will forget that this land was once a place of plenitude."

"What should I do?" asked Apophis.

"Highness, may I walk in your gardens to consider?"

Apophis graciously gestured toward the doorway that led outside.

It was not long before Joseph returned, saying "Begin now to plan for the hard years by growing and storing vast quantities of grain. If you do this, I have thought of a way that you can use that grain to feed your people even in the midst of famine. During those hard years, you can also use that grain as a way to obtain ownership of all of Egypt's best crop land. At the end of that time, your subjects will be indentured servants working your land and tithing part of their harvest to you."

Apophis stared long and hard at Joseph, taking a new measure of the man. "You impress me, young Joseph," said Apophis. "I knew you were a dreamer of dreams, but now I see that you are also a schemer of schemes. You are a visionary and possessed of a certain presence of being. I have been waiting for some time to meet someone who could help advise me in my affairs of state. I think you are that man."

"The power of seeing dreams is my own," said Joseph. "It is a legacy from my family, which has seen more than its share of visionaries. Yet all that I have comes from Yahweh—the one, true God."

"We have many gods," said Pharaoh.

"With respect, Highness, that is why your people are confused and their spirit is torn."

Thus began a long conversation about faith between Pharaoh and Joseph that would last for many years.

## — 6 —

One day, after Joseph had gained Pharaoh's confidence, he was taken to see the throne room. It was an expansive hall lined with gilded pillars along each side. Strange stone gods peaked out from dark nooks. Sculptures of vipers slithered from the corners, uncoiled down from the vaulted ceiling, and wrapped around the tops of the columns. Men and women with the heads of asps, wolves, jackals, and cats stood erect and lined each side of the hall.

The gilded throne was an elaborate sculpture of polished red marble—an enormous, lifelike sphinx with the body of a lion and the head of Apophis. When Pharaoh was seated in front of the lion's breast, his arms rested on the enormous paws, and the beast's great stone head loomed above him. There was an empty space in the middle of the lion's forehead where something had been removed.

"What is missing from that hole?" asked Joseph, pointing.

"That was our family jewel—the silver scarab with seven gems. It was forged as a third, watchful eye to guard and protect us. The scarab was stolen after it had been in our family for seven generations. What good is a symbol of immortality if your lineage cannot hold onto it?"

"What would it mean to you if someone could restore your family's scarab?" asked Joseph, cautiously.

"What is done, is done," said Apophis. "Why waste time dreaming."

"Highness, may I take your leave," asked Joseph, bowing.

Responding with an agreeable, yet puzzled expression, Apophis waved Joseph out with a casual flip of his hand.

Heart racing, Joseph walked out of Pharaoh's temple house and strode across the city. Several people greeted him but he was focused entirely on his destination. It seemed as if his feet barely touched the ground. When he arrived at the house of Potiphar, Joseph quietly stole along the edge of the limestone wall that enclosed the garden, searching for a crack that had served as his hiding place. Reaching deep into the crevice, his hand closed around a small piece of fabric in which, years ago, on that first day he had arrived at Potiphar's home, he had hurriedly wrapped and hidden the silver scarab from the bottom of the well. Back then he had known that, as their slave, his person and sleeping quarters would be considered public space, not suited for keeping secrets or for storing a jewel, especially one whose mere possession, he suspected, could cost him his life.

When he arrived back at Pharaoh's door, Joseph asked again to be announced. While he waited, he gathered his breath and composure.

"Now, dreamer, what is all of this intrigue!" asked Apophis.

Joseph walked up to the sphinx throne. Then he climbed onto the lion's paws, pulled himself up onto its haunches, and kneeled atop the lion's mane. He reached into his satchel and pulled out the small bundle. As Apophis looked on, astonished, Joseph revealed the scarab from the well and held it aloft for all to see.

Taking the scarab firmly in his hand and positioning it carefully, Joseph pushed it into the open depression between the eyes of the sphinx. It snapped into place like a key, drawn in as if by a force of its own. A perfect fit.

"How did you come by this?" demanded Pharaoh, who pushed forward and grabbed Joseph by the arm as he climbed down from the throne. "Are you also a thief?"

"Fate led me to it. Nothing more," Joseph replied. "When I was seventeen, I was beaten and thrown into an empty well along the road to Canaan. My fingers found this silver beetle buried in the soil at the bottom."

Apophis released Joseph's arm and, for the first time in his life, looked upon another man in wonder. Then he told Joseph a story that no one outside his immediate family could have possibly known.

"Some years ago one of my brothers, in a fit of jealousy, stole the jeweled beetle and fled to the north. Our soldiers pursued him for days before he was overtaken and captured. But he didn't have the scarab and denied that he had removed it. We brought him back to the city. It took several more days of, well, *convincing,* for him to tell us that he had stolen it and dropped it into a well after he heard that we were in pursuit."

"Why is it fashioned of silver?" asked Joseph.

"In this land, silver is far more rare and precious than gold."

"Where is your brother now?"

Pharaoh's lips curled and pinched to form an expression that was something between a smile and a sneer. "We sent him on to an early meeting with his ancestors. Our family has been cursed in the years following his death and the loss of this scarab, plagued by ill will, disease, and death. Wait here," said Pharaoh, who then disappeared into an anteroom.

When Apophis reappeared, something dangled from his hand. He walked over to Joseph and placed a necklace over his head. Hanging from the chain was a pendant—an exact miniature replica of the silver scarab and seven jewels.

"Truly, you are a messenger sent to help my people," he exclaimed, embracing Joseph. "From this day forward, you will serve as the vizier of this house, second in command over all that I rule."

That evening after the late day meal, Apophis walked with Joseph among the elaborate gardens that surrounded the house of Pharaoh. They strolled beneath date palms and cedars, bay and box trees. Joseph's senses basked in the florid air, tinged by the aromas of hyssop and myrtle, algum, and cassia. They passed trees and flowers that Joseph had never seen, whose seeds had been gathered from distant lands and purchased at great cost. For the first time, Joseph spoke at length about his family's history, and their deep, longstanding faith in Yahweh.

# — 7 —

The next seven years were times of unrivaled abundance, just as Joseph had foreseen. These years saw Joseph's final stages of initiation and acceptance into Egyptian society. He was now clothed in the finest linens embellished with gold. He learned how to move adroitly through the tangled web of society, among the ruling class, without getting ensnared by those who were always waiting to reap the spoils that came to those who felled the mighty. During those years of rich harvest, Joseph became a familiar sight as he moved about the city and countryside in his chariot. During each harvest, he arranged to have vast quantities of grain gathered and stored in the pharaoh's granaries—voluminous dunes of wheat, rye, and barley.

Now in his early thirties, Joseph courted a wife from within Egypt's high society. He attended many of the most exclusive social affairs, and his romantic inclinations were the source of endless speculation, particularly because, unlike most men, he shunned any association with courtesans. Joseph had become adept at plucking these vibrations of gossip and intrigue like the strings of a lyre. To him, it was like the games of chance he once played with the guards at the prison tower, with the goal of bluffing others while he, alone, knew his true hand. Joseph was subtle but persistent as he deftly pursued his desires.

At one social gathering, on a sultry summer evening, Joseph was strolling through the pharaoh's beloved hanging gardens. The familiar scent of gardenia, which Joseph had often thought of as being overly sweet, tonight smelled of new possibilities. Hand in hand he walked with Asenath of Heliopolis, the daughter of Potiphera, chief priest of On, and worshiper of the sun god, Ra. Asenath, whose name meant "of the Goddess Neith," was a scion from the lineage of the Egyptian spiritual leaders. Tall, dark, and voluptuous, she was considered by many to be the most beautiful woman they had ever beheld. Her full lips, obsidian eyes, and sloping forehead gave her a regal air that befit her bloodline. On this night, she wore a delicate headband from which a teardrop-shaped pendant of polished lapis dangled in the space between her wide-set eyes. Her stylish sandals turned up to form a graceful arc in front of her toes.

Later that evening, Joseph found himself standing on the edge of Pharaoh's ornate portico, with an arm around his lover's waist. She leaned into him, and he inhaled the lingering scent of rose. One of the pharaoh's cats began to weave its way around their ankles, purring loudly. Asenath reached down and petted its soft fur, admiring the refined lines of its body, the sleek black face and ears.

There, arrayed below them in all of its splendor and moonlit allure, they looked out from a height that revealed the hills of the city.

"I was born here and have lived in this place all my life," said Asenath wistfully. "This is all I have ever known."

"Then you shall have it," said Joseph with a wry smile.

"What? Have you now become Pharaoh?" teased Asenath. "That is a grand thought for one who comes from a family of … what did you say the other night … shepherds?"

She nudged him in the side, then began to finger the scarab amulet that hung around his neck. Joseph inhaled the rich, fruity scent of wine on her breath.

"And you, my love, do you have something against shepherds?"

"Not as long as they know how to fight off the wolves," she whispered in his ear. She looked up at his face then and wondered if it was the low, ruddy moon or if the great and feared vizier was flush with indignation.

Joseph gathered himself, tightened his grip around one of the intricately carved ebony pillars, then said. "My father, and his father before, *were* shepherds, love. But look at what I have become." Gesturing out across the verge before them, he said in a somewhat raised voice that was just loud enough for those in the crowd to hear who stood with bended ear, "These people are now my flock, Asenath. I have become a shepherd of men."

Egypt's most celebrated young couple in a generation were wed when the groves of olive trees were adorned with pink and white blossoms, harbingers of the fruit that would be pressed into oil and scented for the pharaoh's daily ablutions. Joseph adored Asenath for both her beauty and her spirit. In their new marriage, he saw his life meld with that of the great house of Potiphera. His was a driving passion. When he stared into her eyes, he seemed to focus in the distance; he saw beyond their love to a farther destiny. She was the key to his door, which opened into a future that he had already dreamed.

When their first son was born, Joseph saw in his eyes the promise of new beginnings that somehow prompted him to reflect on his own past. "I will call him Manasseh," he said to Asenath, "because by his birth he has made me forget some of the pain and suffering I have endured with my own family."

Shortly after that, Asenath again became pregnant. As she began to swell with child, Joseph teased her. "You are my pomegranate," he would say. "You are my ripe date."

One day Asenath replied, "Yes, Husband, and I grew this fruit from your seed. So, what does that make you? An almond? A pistachio? Or just any kind of nut."

Sensing that there was a joust to her jest, Joseph asked, "How do you mean?"

"You always did have a thick shell."

"Is that right?" asked Joseph, half amused.

"Yes, and you are good at storing yourself away for long periods of time."

"That's because I'm saving myself for you, dear," he said, thinking he'd won the last retort.

"Just take care, dear, that you don't dry out and shrivel up in the meanwhile," she jibed.

About a year after Manasseh was born, Asenath had another boy. "We are so blessed," she said to Joseph as they looked upon their newborn. "Let us call him Ephraim, 'he has made me fruitful.'"

# — 8 —

Joseph's youth had embedded hardship in his marrow. He was a stoical leader. Many called him heartless. When locusts swarmed and ate the last good crop of the plentiful years, he was more than ready: he had been waiting and planning for seven years. When the heat and dry winds blew in from the east and famine finally struck his adopted homeland, he rediscovered keen instincts for turning tragedy into triumph.

Step by step, Joseph created an empire by using the immense stores of grain that he had amassed for Apophis during the seven years of plenty. When families had no more grain to make bread, they came to Joseph and traded their livestock and horses for bread to last a year. After that food was gone, Joseph offered them grain for their land. Faced with either a painful parting of their family's legacy, or starvation, there was no choice. In time, Pharaoh owned all of the best crop land in Egypt. But the famine was unrelenting; it howled at their doors like a pack of ravenous wolves. The only thing that the people of Egypt had left to give was their labor and freedom. They agreed to accept survival rations of grain as barter for working what was now the pharaoh's land in exchange for one-fifth of every harvest. As the years of famine dragged mercilessly on, Joseph's cold, elegant plan spun a ruthless web that ensnared all of Egypt's most fertile lands and indentured her people to a lifetime of serfdom.

---

Famine also struck in Canaan, the land of Joseph's family. Israel heard that Egypt was the only place where quantities of grain could still be found for purchase.

"We have no choice," he said to his sons. "Go to the land of Pharaoh and buy what we need. The famine will not last forever, but we have to do what we must until then. Reuben and Judah, organize your brothers and set off as soon as you can."

"Everyone?" asked Judah.

Ever since Israel had been told that Joseph was dead, he took no chances with his other son by Rachel. "Benjamin, the youngest among you, will remain here where I know he is safe."

The next morning, Joseph's brothers began the long trek to Egypt. Traveling lightly by camel, the ten men moved swiftly. They followed the southern coast of the Great Sea, forded the Stream of Egypt, and rode the waves of dried grassland that encrusted the vast Wilderness of Shur. On through the brittle shrublands they rode, skirting the southern shore of Lake Menzaleh. Slowed by fatigue and a paucity of water, they passed through the land of Goshen, came to the upper reaches of the Nile delta, and pushed south through the heat, dust, and languid desert air.

Many days after their journey had begun, they at last entered the city, plodding along and spent. Soon a chariot drawn by horses came thundering toward them.

"*Abrek, abrek!*" commanded the driver. "Make way!"

Aroused from their lassitude, Joseph's brothers stepped to the side of the road just as the chariot drew up with a pounding of hooves, enveloping them in a swirling cloud of dust.

"Follow me," said the driver, who, without waiting for a reply, turned around and drove back from whence he had come.

The chariot led them to the house of Apophis. There they were given water, food, and a place to bathe. Then all ten brothers were led into an ornate room where the vizier was waiting.

"Who is that?" whispered Simeon.

"Perhaps it is Pharaoh," answered Reuben.

"I don't like the looks of him," said Dan.

Standing before them was a tall, muscular man who wore a kind of tunic that covered him from the waist down. His perfectly proportioned chest muscles suggested one whose form is the result of exercise designed for sculpting, rather than a product of hard work. A kind of leather belt was fastened around his forehead, deeply tooled to appear like two enfolding wings. The necklace that hung around his neck bore a silver scarab that was inlaid with a glittering piece of onyx—the pharaoh's seal.

Joseph knew his brothers at once. Yet he had grown and changed so dramatically since they had last seen him at the age of seventeen that they didn't recognize him.

In a deep voice, Joseph asked "Who are you and why have you come here? Only spies would travel in such great numbers and with so few belongings. But if you are spies, you are incompetent. My men saw you coming from far off."

As he stood in the ensuing silence, Joseph caught the eyes of every one of his brothers. He searched for a sign of recognition, but found none.

"Highness, we are not spies," said Judah at last. "We have come from the land of Canaan. The famine has now reached our families. Our father has sent us to trade for grain. We have ample payment to offer."

Joseph's guard began to drop when he heard that Israel was still alive. He wanted to step down and ask, "How is our father? Does he remember me well?" But he caught himself and girded his resolve all the more. Joseph's anger toward his brothers was still strong.

"Is this all of your men?" asked Joseph.

Before Reuben could stop him, Gad said, "No, our youngest brother remains at home."

"Throw them into the cells of the stone tower!" Joseph commanded his guards.

After they were led away, Joseph retired alone to the garden. He sat beneath an ancient cedar, bent his head, and wept. His heart was breaking to see Israel and his one true brother, Benjamin.

In three days' time, his brothers were again brought before Joseph.

"I have reconsidered," said Joseph. "The bags on your camels and donkeys have been loaded with grain. Payment was taken from the money we found in your belongings. Now return to your father's house and bring me your youngest brother. But this one will remain with me as an assurance," said Joseph pointing to Simeon.

They left for Canaan at once. That evening, as Joseph's nine brothers set up camp for the night, Issachar yelled, "Look at this, my money has been stowed in a sack of grain. They have sent us back with the grain *and* our money."

"This is a setup," said Levi. "They're trying to make us out as thieves."

Naphtali said, "We should return it immediately."

"Patience, brothers," said Reuben. "If Levi is right, the vizier's men would have been upon us as soon as we left the city. Some other plan is at work here."

"But is it a plan of men or an act of Yahweh?" posed Judah.

"We will have to wait and see," said Reuben. "We continue on in the morning."

— 9 —

When those nine sons of Israel's arrived home, they told their father what had happened and what the vizier had demanded.

Israel tore his shirt in despair, "Joseph is dead and Simeon is now a prisoner in Pharaoh's house. I will never agree to send Benjamin back with you for risk of losing him as well. If their mother, Rachel, were here, she would pull out her hair at the thought of it."

"But Father," pleaded Judah, "think of Simeon. We have to get him back."

"Here is what we are going to do," Israel said. "Load up your satchels with twice the money that you first paid Pharaoh for the wheat. We will all go to Egypt with Benjamin. Then we will trade the money for Simeon and be gone."

They passed through Beersheba on the way back to Egypt. Once they had prepared camp for the night, Israel walked off a short distance from the tents and sat down to pray near a small juniper. While he sat in silence looking up at the sky, the stars began to move and spiral, closer and closer, until they became a sphere of shimmering white light in the heavens. Then, Yahweh spoke to Israel for the last time.

"Have faith, Israel, for I will go with you into Egypt. In that land you will be the father of a great nation. The last face you see before you come to me will be that of your beloved son, Joseph." Israel told no one of his vision.

Many days later, they came again to the outskirts of the city.

"Father, we cannot risk having you fall into the hands of Pharaoh. Stay here in these hills with one of the servants. If we return and blow the horn of the ibex, only then will it be safe to come out and meet us."

Later that day, when they again found themselves in the great hall, Reuben spoke to the vizier.

"As you have commanded, Highness, here is our youngest brother. Now, please return our brother Simeon. These losses that have come to pass are breaking our father's heart. He is an old man and has suffered much in his years."

Moved almost to tears over Israel's grief and with a burning desire to see his father, Joseph tempered his will. "As you wish, for you have done what I asked of you. As an act of hospitality, I will send you home with as much food as you can carry."

Joseph was afraid he would never see his father again. As the servants filled his brothers' panniers with grain, Joseph hid one of his silver cups in Benjamin's portion.

The next morning, Israel's sons fled the city at nearly a full gallop despite the heavy load their animals bore. But just as they approached the place where Israel was hiding, they heard the heavy drumbeat of hooves in pursuit.

Riding in horse-drawn chariots, Joseph and his men caught up with them and began to search Benjamin's satchel of grain.

"What is this?" bellowed Joseph as he pulled the silver cup from Benjamin's satchel. "Is this how you show your gratitude? I should have you all put to death for robbing from the pharaoh."

"I did not take the cup!" Benjamin protested. "It is some kind of trick!"

"For that insolence, you will become Pharaoh's slave. Be off with the rest of you before I change my mind and decide to leave your bones for the vultures."

"At that moment, Asher raised the ibex horn to his lips. Its clarion sound rang out and echoed in the nearby hills.

Reuben strode up to Asher and reproached him beneath his breath. "What have you done? Now you have also put our father at risk!"

Answering the signal, a single camel and rider, led by a servant at the reins, sauntered toward them from where they had been hiding in the folds of that barren land.

"Hah!" Joseph exclaimed sarcastically. "Are these your rein-forcements?"

The camel stopped close to Joseph. Asher helped an old man to dismount whose head was covered with a hood to protect him from the sun. Israel shambled forward as Joseph dismounted to meet this mysterious stranger.

Israel walked up to Joseph and uncovered his head. When Joseph saw the face of his father, an expression of deep sadness came over him. Tears streamed from his eyes, and his shoulders were wracked with sobs.

"Father," said Joseph.

Israel began to shudder. He fell to his knees and looked to the sky in doubt.

"What cruel cunning is this that a stranger would mock the grief of an old man! This son died more than twenty years ago!"

Joseph gently lifted Israel to his feet and steadied the old man before him, who looked all of his one hundred and thirty years. "Father, look. It is me, Joseph."

"Who calls me father?"

"Your son, Joseph."

His eyes strained. "Is that truly you?"

"Yes, Father."

"My son," said Israel as his eyes glazed over and he embraced him. "How I have missed you."

Israel then stepped back from Joseph to look at him. Gazing up, Israel saw the eyes of his beloved Rachel for the first time in more than twenty years. "My dear, dear boy," he said, abandoning himself to a wave of joy tempered only by a lingering sense of what had been lost. Israel cried freely. "Joseph," he said, reaching out again with both arms and kissing him profusely on the forehead and cheeks. "Praise Yahweh, my son has been delivered from the dead!"

"Not exactly, Father. I have been living here in Egypt for all these years. Come, ride with me. There is much to tell."

As they rode into the city together, Joseph basked in the paternal love that he had thought was lost forever. With Israel at his side, the compassion and protection that Joseph felt for his father unfurled as a great tent that sheltered his brothers from the anger Joseph still harbored in a dark corner of his heart.

# — 10 —

Joseph sent word to Apophis that his family had arrived from Canaan. By the following evening, a lavish meal had been prepared to welcome them.

As they entered the dining hall, Joseph's brothers trailed behind while he helped Israel forward to meet Apophis. When they came together, Israel bowed as well as his old, creaking bones would allow. Then Joseph witnessed Pharaoh do something he had never seen: Apophis bowed to another person.

"Highness, I am grateful for your hospitality," said Joseph as he ushered his eleven brothers into Pharaoh's great hall. After introductions were made, they took their seats and prepared to partake of the most lavish banquet any of them had seen in years. The two great men sat beside each other at the table.

"Tell me, Israel—father of Joseph—how many journeys of the sun have you seen?" asked Apophis.

"By my count, one hundred and thirty."

"And have they been good years?"

"Most have," said Israel. "The difficult years came in our times of wandering the desert. The hardest when my loved ones have died. But the most magnificent time is upon me now, finding again my living son Joseph and seeing his success in this great land of Pharaoh."

"You are most kind," said Apophis.

"I offer you my blessing," said Israel as he lifted his silver chalice of wine. When everyone had raised their chalices, he continued, "May your people endure this time of hardship and live to prosper again in this land."

As they resumed their conversations, such a tantalizing bouquet of aromas drifted into the room that their mouths began to water before the meal arrived.

First came some small silver bowls that held a mix of dates, nuts, figs, and mango. Then they were served soft, warm circles of unleavened bread on which they spread a smooth, strong butter made from goat's milk. The scent of coriander filled the room as the main course of spiced lentils, soft cheese, and tender flanks from a freshly killed steer was brought to the table. In between each course, the guests were offered stalks of anise to clear the palate and prepare for the next dish. Dessert was a rich, dark carob pudding spiced with a hint of cumin. At the end of the meal, each guest was given a small piece of a cleansing gum to chew, which was made from the thick sap of the mastic tree.

"I have never tasted such a repast," said Israel as he leaned back in contentment.

"You have been most generous to prepare this fine feast," said Joseph.

"It was nothing," granted Apophis, as he motioned for the servants to clear the table. "Now, I have arranged for a caravan of wagons to return with you to Canaan in the morning."

An uneasy silence came over the hall. Everyone's eyes were on Apophis.

"No, no, you misunderstand me!" said Apophis. "Go back to Canaan to collect your families and gather your belongings. Then return to live here. I am granting you some of the finest land in Egypt. We are only in the second year of the famine, and I would have Joseph's family well provided for during the remaining time of scarcity."

Joseph helped his family to prepare. Donkeys were loaded with food. Each person was given a colorful, flowing robe of the kind that was usually worn for celebrations. Joseph gave his younger brother,

Benjamin, a full wardrobe cut from the finest cloth, plus a large sum of three hundred shekels of silver.

"But you, Father, you will remain here with me and wait for their return," said Joseph to Israel. Your days of traveling across the desert are over."

Several weeks passed. One day, a guard who patrolled the outskirts of Pharaoh's palace came riding in. "There appears to be a small city of people and animals moving toward us, coming out of the north and east."

Joseph led Israel up the stairs to a high point of the temple walls. "See, Father, there is your nation, come to live with you. Everyone is arriving. They have brought oxen and asses, donkeys and sheep. What a sight! Look, people are gathering all around the eastern edge of the city to watch them arrive."

Standing in that high place next to the firstborn son of Rachel, seeing the great procession as it approached through the heat and rustle, Israel pictured the faces of all his children and their spouses, his grandchildren and great-grandchildren. There was the house of Israel on the move, stretching to the horizon, entering a new land. He swelled with pride and satisfaction—a joy deeper than any he had ever known or imagined.

"If ever your faith should waver, remember what you have seen this day," said Israel, his mind expansive. "Those are the faces of your kinfolk. They are a tide unto themselves, rising into the land of Pharaoh. Here is living proof of Yahweh's promise."

## — 11 —

Israel's people settled their flocks in Goshen, atop the rich alluvial soil on the eastern edge of the Nile delta. Years passed. The famine burned the land as a fire consumes its fuel. When Joseph's seemingly endless stores of grain began to run low, the rains at last returned. For the first time in seven long years, Egypt bloomed with an ocean of flowers that brushed the hills with waves of color like none could recall. A few moons into the greening of the land, the crops again began to bear. The first harvest after the famine saw the return of a time when food was plentiful.

Time flowed. Israel was now an ancient who had seen one hundred and forty-seven years. His health was failing.

"My son of Rachel ..." he said to Joseph one day.

"Yes, Father," Joseph replied, knowing that his father only referred to him that way when he was about to broach something important.

"I have told you of how your mother was taken from me, and that we buried her there by the road between Mamre and beth El."

"Yes, Father."

"Soon after that time, El Shaddai spoke to me and said that my descendants would be as many as the stars. Now bring your two sons to me."

In a short while, Joseph returned with Manasseh and Ephraim. His two oldest sons were now close to the age that Joseph had been when he arrived in Egypt.

194

Hearing them approach, Israel said, "Bring them closer for I cannot see."

When the two boys stood by his bed, Israel asked, "Who are these two standing here."

"They are my sons, Manasseh and Ephraim."

Israel hugged and kissed each of them in turn, then he said, "Come, sit here between my legs."

Joseph understood that this meant Israel was about to adopt his two sons as his own, which would bestow a great honor and fortune upon them. He led each young man over and motioned for them to sit on the bed. Ephraim was seated on Israel's left and Manasseh, the older, on his right. Joseph knew that a blessing with the right hand was a powerful omen of good fortune.

But Israel crossed his hands before placing them on the brother's heads, so that his right hand lay on the head of Ephraim.

"No, no, Father," said Joseph, pulling at Israel's hand. "Manasseh is the older son. Please, put your right hand on his head. Here, let me help you."

Israel yanked his right hand free and again rested it on Ephraim, saying, "Let go, Joseph. I know what I am doing. Manasseh will lead a good life and have a family as well. But Ephraim is going to husband a great people."

Then Israel blessed them, saying, "Yahweh showed mercy to Abraham and Isaac before me, and I have been protected by angels. You, Manasseh, and you Ephraim, are our gifts from God and our forefathers. May Yahweh bring you many blessings that your descendants will carry our name to a multitude. And may God guide you so that others will call upon your names as a blessing on their people."

"Thank you, Grandfather," said Ephraim and Manasseh. Then they stood, bowed to Israel, and left his bedside.

When they were gone, Israel turned to Joseph and said, "Son, I wish to bless you now."

Joseph knew that his father was preparing to die. He sat next to his bed and took Israel's hand. As the sound of his father's voice washed over him, Joseph recalled what they had shared together: how he had ridden on his father's shoulders along the dusty desert trails, the time they had played in the vineyard of his grandfather Isaac's. Tears of both joy and sadness slid down his cheeks and dripped off the tip of his chin.

"Joseph, come here now and place your hand on my groin," said Israel.

After Joseph had done this, Israel said, "Swear to me that you will lay me to rest in the tomb of our forebears, in the cave at Machpelah, near where once grew the great Oak of Mamre, that there I will lie, by the side of those who have gone before me, Abraham and Sarah, Isaac and Rebekah, and where I buried my wife Leah many years ago."

"I swear it, Father."

When Joseph emerged from the room, each of Israel's children came in turn, from oldest to youngest, and sat by Israel's side as he intoned a blessing: Reuben, Simeon, Levi, Judah, Dan, Naphtali, Gad, Asher, Issachar, Zebulun, Dinah, and Benjamin.

Israel called again for Joseph, who came and stood by his side. Now Israel, once Jacob, looked up toward heaven. He reached out his hands and made the motions of someone climbing. His eyes opened wide as if he were cresting a tall mountain and seeing a beautiful land that lay beyond for the first time. Then his arms sank back onto the bed and the light drained from his eyes, but his face was fixed in the expression of one who has beheld great beauty.

# — 12 —

After Israel's sons returned from burying their father, Joseph again became distant. He completely removed himself from their lives. Now that his father was gone, the anger that he had felt toward his brothers—which had quietly smoldered during Israel's time in Egypt—flared up once again. The harder he struggled against this powerful force, the more his mind began to twist with the vengeful thoughts of old. Over time, his hateful notions grew into possibilities, which matured into a plot.

One day, Joseph summoned his older brothers to the great hall. Ten guards ushered them in and forcibly arranged them in an arc facing Joseph. One guard stood directly behind each brother.

Joseph waited at the top of a flight of seven steps. He was standing erect, with his hands behind his back.

"Brothers, now that our father, Israel, has passed, the sands have again shifted, and they do not drift in your favor."

"What would you have us do?" asked Simeon.

"Silence!" demanded Joseph. "You always mocked my dreams. Now you will watch as something I have dreamt of doing for a long time becomes your own nightmare. Reuben, it was your idea to throw me in the well. Come forward."

Reuben walked toward him and stood at the bottom of the stone steps.

"As you are aware, my love for Israel has been your shield. Now that our father has died, it is again just between us."

Issachar begged, "Please, Brother, spare our lives. On our honor, we will leave here and never return."

"Up here, Brother," said Joseph in a voice that would not be denied, as he pointed to the step just below where he was standing. Reuben climbed and stood before him.

Slowly, Joseph brought his hands around in front, revealing that he held an old, wizened camel-skin pouch. As he opened the hide, it creaked and split from age. Reaching into it, Joseph pulled out a knife.

"Do you recognize this knife?" asked Joseph, holding it out before him.

Everyone strained to see, then shook their heads.

"And this?" asked Joseph holding aloft the scabbard.

Slowly, a look of recognition, then of amazement, came over Judah's face.

"Yes, yes!" he said. "The oak-leaf hilt of gold. A ram's-horn handle and an ivory scabbard carved as a ring dove in flight. It cannot be!"

"See and believe!" said Joseph.

Everyone looked around and spoke in hushed voices.

"But … but I thought that knife only existed in myth," said Zebulun.

Joseph pulled off the ivory sheath and exposed the glistening blade. Immediately, and with the heartless sound of sharpened metal sliding from scabbards, the ten guards bared their swords. Joseph's brothers stiffened. Shivers ran along their spines. Sweat beaded up and dripped down their faces.

Joseph turned the sharp edge of the knife toward Reuben's throat.

"Please, don't!" said Reuben.

"And why not?" Joseph demanded.

"What we did to you—that was long ago."

"Time remembers. It does not forgive," said Joseph.

"Then, for Israel, to honor the love you still hold in your heart for our father, and that he had for you."

Joseph hesitated. He looked out at his brothers, sweeping his eyes around the arc in which they were arrayed, meeting the frightened gaze of each in turn. His hand still held the knife, poised at Reuben's throat.

At that instant, there came a clatter of footsteps upon the stones by the entry. Reuben's wife rushed in, chasing his two-year-old son, Zapeth.

"I'm sorry, Reuben," she said, before looking up. "He was impatient and got away from me." She stooped down and picked up Zapeth, then stood and gasped as she took in the scene in the great hall.

As shock gave way to understanding, she cried out in a voice that caused everyone to wince. "No, no, no, Joseph. Please, oh, *no*! Reuben is the one who saved your life at the well. He told me what happened."

When Joseph turned his gaze toward her, he saw little Zapeth's shining, uncomprehending eyes fixed upon him and the knife in his hand, watching intently and as innocently as if they were gathered to play some mysterious game.

"My youngest son," whispered Reuben, the movement causing the knife to cut his skin. A trickle of blood began to run down his neck.

The muscles in Joseph's knife hand relaxed, and he withdrew it from Reuben's throat. Then the lines of his face softened, and his shoulders rounded. He slipped the blade back into its ivory sheath. His brothers could hear the swords behind them carefully sliding into their scabbards. A collective sigh arose, as if the room itself had begun to breathe again.

Tears welled up in Joseph's eyes, and his brow rucked into a look of anguish.

"Joseph, forgive us," said Reuben. "We were just a pack of young, jealous fools."

Looking out at his brothers now, the warmth of compassion slowly came into Joseph's eyes. The ring that had constricted his heart was finally loosening—the one that was forged in the heat of rage and tempered by a sense of righteous injustice many years ago.

Unexpectedly, Joseph again pulled himself up to his full height. With a deft movement that startled Reuben and brought him to his knees and caused everyone in the room to flinch, Joseph suddenly brought his arm straight up as if stabbing the sky. His voice echoed in the vast hall, shaking the pillars to their footings.

"Behold the Knife of the Covenant. This is the blade of our father, Jacob, of Isaac before him, and back through the centuries to our patriarch, Abraham. It is the symbol of our forefathers' faith and pledge to Yahweh."

The room was silent but for Zapeth's muted cooings.

"Our forebears have honored the covenant for four long generations, through hardship and pain, ecstasy and love. We are the fruit of that covenant. We are the stars in the sky that guided them in the darkness. We are the grains of sand that blew through the time of our people's journeys across the desert. We are the specks of dust that came to inherit the land of our fathers. We are Yahweh's promise fulfilled!"

"Hold out your left hand," Joseph said to Reuben.

Reuben slowly put his hand forward. Joseph grabbed hard onto his brother's wrist, took the tip of the knife, and etched a clean cut across his palm. Reuben grimaced and tightened his jaw as thick blood oozed from the wound.

Before Reuben could pull back, Joseph held up his own left hand and, with one deft flick of the blade, angled a cut along the life line of his palm.

"Step up here with me and give me your hand!" Joseph demanded.

When Reuben rose and held out his hand, Joseph grasped it firmly so that their bleeding palms pressed tightly together.

As Joseph raised their clasped hands, warm crimson dripped and splattered onto the polished, alabaster steps at their feet.

Joseph held the knife aloft in his other hand. With both arms raised high, he looked out to address his brothers, and said, "This blood is the bond of the covenant, the living symbol of our forefathers' faith and sacrifice."

In a deep, sonorous voice that filled their hearts with hope, Joseph exclaimed, "What Yahweh has joined, let no one tear asunder!"

# Reader's Questions and
# Topics for Discussion

## Abram and Sarai

• Abram and Sarai lived four thousand years ago. What issues did Abram and Sarai face during their lifetimes that are the same as or different than the issues that couples now experience?

• How do Abram and Sarai respond to being childless? Do people today consider infertility a matter of faith? What choices do we have that they did not? What are the spiritual and ethical implications of these choices?

• Why would Yahweh appear to Abram by an ancient tree? In what other places does Yahweh appear to people in the wild? Why do you think this happens so often?

• During the famine, Abram offers his wife to Pharaoh Amenemhet. Sarai agrees to the arrangement. How does this experience affect their marriage? What happens to move them beyond that wounded place?

• What is the meaning of Abram's blood offering to Yahweh? What do the flames symbolize that appear in between the halves of the slaughtered animals ?

• Why would Yahweh choose circumcision to be the mark of the covenant with Abram and his people? What is Yahweh's promise to Abram?

• Abraham questions Yahweh's intent toward the town of Sodom. How does Yahweh respond to this challenge?

- Abimelech, king of Gerar, is a classic example of someone who is caught up in circumstances that are not of his doing, but which have a profound affect on his life. How does he respond? What would you have done in his place? Does his situation remind you of that of any other person in the Bible?

- When Isaac begins to grow up, why does Sarah turn against Hagar and Ishmael. What is her motive? What else could she have done? How does this event help determine who Ishmael becomes?

- Why would Yahweh ask Abraham to sacrifice Isaac, his only son by Sarah, then have an angel spare Isaac's life at the last moment? How does Abraham transform this experience into a turning point that comes to symbolize his covenant with Yahweh?

- Has your own faith ever been tested by an event that was beyond anything you had previously imagined? What happened? How did you respond?

- When Sarah dies, Abraham buries her with a scarf that symbolizes the ring dove. What did that bird mean to Sarah during her lifetime?

### Isaac and Rebekah

- What does Isaac's relationship to the natural world mean to him? How does it affect the way in which he lives his life?

- Why do so many people feel close to God when they are in the presence of nature? Has this been your experience? Where do you feel the presence of God?

- Given the customs of the time, why do the sons of Abraham and Isaac marry into their extended families?

- Eliezer chooses a potential wife for Isaac by testing the generosity of the women who come to the well. What other stories can you recall in which an important event begins by someone passing a crucial test? Why is this such a common theme?

- Isaac's life with Rebekah begins just after he sees his reflection in the water at Lahai Roi, the Well of the Seeing Spirit. Why do so many turning points in these stories revolve around wells?

- The theme of trying and failing to conceive children until late in life pervades these stories. Why do you think Yahweh chooses to form bonds of faith around promising to provide many descendants for these biblical families? Why is raising a large family not as important to many couples in our times?

- What do the birds of prey represent in the battle of the skies between Isaac's eagle and Ishmael's falcon, Anakim? How do these birds symbolize the character of each man?

- Yahweh offers gifts to Isaac because Abraham kept his faith. How did Abraham live a life of faith?

- The oasis where Isaac and Rebekah discover the Knife of the Covenant is a metaphor for the spiritual root of Abraham's bind. What does it represent?

- Over the years, carvings and elements were added to complete the Knife of the Covenant. What is the meaning of each figure?

- What complementary aspects of our beings do Jacob and Esau represent?

- Why does Rebekah help Jacob obtain his father's blessing, even at the expense of her firstborn son, Esau?

### Jacob, Rachel, and Leah

- Jacob's life is transformed by his prophetic vision of light as he flees across the desert. Since few of us ever experience such a clear and profound vision, what can we look for as signs to guide our way?

- Eliezer discovers Rebekah at her local well in Haran. Later, Rebekah's son Jacob meets Rachel at the well outside the city of Paddan-aram. In that time and region, wells were an important gathering place for the local community. What places serve a similar purpose in contemporary society? What is a common expression for a gathering place that may have its origins in these times?

- What object of importance did Rebekah pack at the bottom of Jacob's satchel? Why did she do so? What was she really passing on to Jacob?

- From the very start, Jacob's uncle Laban starts planning ways to take advantage of his nephew's desire to marry Rachel. Why does Laban trick Jacob into marrying his older daughter, Leah? What is his ultimate motive?

- How does Jacob respond to Laban's deceit in a way that reveals his own growth and maturity? As a shepherd, what does Jacob use to outwit his uncle's scheming?

- How does the sibling rivalry between Rachel and Leah affect how their children are treated? Who is favored and why? How does this set the stage for the far-reaching events that are yet to come?

- Why does Rachel steal the heirlooms of Laban's family before she flees across the desert with Jacob, Leah, and the children? What is she really taking? Do you think that Jacob knows she has possession of the heirlooms when Laban and his men search their camp?

- When Jacob wrestles with a supernatural being at Peniel, he is physically wrestling with God. It is considered certain death to see the face of God (Exodus 33:20) unless by divine intervention. What does this event reveal about the importance God places upon Jacob and his future role?

- Esau's joyous greeting of Jacob in the desert after twenty years of separation is one of the great acts of forgiveness in the Bible. How does this event foreshadow what is to come? How could things have gone differently if Esau had not forgiven his brother for stealing Isaac's blessing? What other generous acts of forgiveness in faith and history have come to shape the world we live in?

- When Jacob's family reaches the altar at beth El, which he had made twenty years earlier, he has everyone add a new stone. Why does he do this? What does it teach the children about faith and about family?

- After Rachel dies, Jacob raises a pillar to mark her grave along the road from beth El to Ephrath. (This stone still stands and is now know as the Pillar of Rachel's Grave.) Then Jacob wanders out into the desert, overcome with grief over the loss of his beloved. Why does Yahweh reveal to Jacob the vision in the stars at that particular moment of his anguish?

## Joseph

- At one point in the story, Joseph reveals the source of his dreams. Where does he say they come from?

- How do Joseph's dreams set events in motion that are beyond Joseph's control? What role do dreams continue to play throughout his life?

- From where do you believe your dreams arise? Do you ever have dreams that help to guide your decisions or the direction of your life?

- Over time, Joseph is faced with many challenges: his brothers' betrayal, the false accusations of Potiphar's wife, the jealous rage of Potiphar himself, and the early suspicions of Pharaoh Apophis. Each time, Joseph prevails, emerging from the well, from servitude to Potiphar, and even from imprisonment in the round stone tower of the prison. How is Joseph able to turn adversity into opportunity? Which gifts does he receive that he uses to his advantage? What aspects of his character does he draw from to succeed?

- When Israel is told that his beloved son Joseph is dead, he wanders off into the night in tears and anguish and implores Yahweh, "Why—after I have prayed and kept faith for all these long years? Why?" How can we keep faith at times when circumstances are harsh and painful and life seems unjust?

- Pharaoh Apophis comes to see Joseph as a man of destiny. What convinces Apophis that Joseph is a man of wisdom—a powerful ally who can help to guide and advance Pharaoh's rule over Egypt?

- Joseph finds a scarab amulet in the bottom of the well, an image that was both powerful and popular in Egypt during Joseph's lifetime. What does the scarab amulet signify in the lineage of Pharaoh Apophis? What does it come to symbolize in the evolution of Joseph's life?

- Joseph's scheme for feeding people during the famine saves their lives, but it also forces the growers to deed their land to Pharaoh and indentures future generations to servitude in

Egypt. What does this grand plan reveal about the complex nature of Joseph, a man of compassion and cunning?

- The famine in Egypt lasts for seven years—a significant number that recurs throughout the Bible. Where else in the Bible does the number seven appear? In what other stories do you recall finding the number seven? Why do you think this number is so significant?

- In the land of Egypt, Joseph toys with his brothers as a cat would with a mouse. Who, in Joseph's past, left him this legacy of tricking others? What do Joseph's overt games reveal about the conflicted way he feels toward his brothers? With what feelings does he struggle? Have you ever felt strongly conflicted feelings toward someone in your family? How do you reconcile those feelings?

- Joseph's reunion with his father, Israel, marks a point of personal transformation. What does this pivotal moment reveal about Joseph's ultimate values?

- Even after Joseph was betrayed by his older brothers, he still feels compassion toward his father, Israel, and his younger brother, Benjamin. How does this compassion influence his ultimate decision about the fate of his older brothers?

- What does the little child Zapeth, who is Reuben's youngest son, represent for Joseph during the crucial moment of decision when he holds his brothers' lives in the balance?

- In the end, what does Joseph do with the Knife of the Covenant that proves his faith to Yahweh? How does this compare with what Joseph's grandfather Isaac did with the Knife to prove *his* faith?

# Acknowledgments

In both mind and spirit, I left home for weeks on end while writing this book—galloping across the desert over breakfast, plotting elements of a story when I was out for a walk, conversing with biblical characters while riding alone in the car. I could not have done so without the unequivocal support of my wife, Marie Levesque Caduto, who tolerated my many absences and helped me to keep an eye on a further range. Marie also provided insightful comments on the evolving manuscript.

My gratitude to Stuart M. Matlins, publisher of SkyLight Paths, for believing in this project, and to the editorial team of Mark Ogilbee, project editor; Maura D. Shaw, senior development editor; and Emily Wichland, vice president of editorial and production. Mark Ogilbee also acted as the vigilant shepherd, gently guiding the creative process toward greener pastures. Lauren Seidman and Sarah McBride, project editors, smoothed the way from manuscript to book, and Sara Dismukes, book and cover designer, crafted the elegant look and feel of the final volume.

My profound appreciation to the people and places that appear in this book: lives and landscapes that spoke so clearly to me through time and space. Finally, none of this would have been possible without the gift of faith in God, which guides my own wanderings in mysterious ways.

# About the Author

Michael J. Caduto is a renowned author, educator and storyteller who has written and coauthored fifteen books, including the Keepers of the Earth series, *In the Beginning: The Story of Genesis and Earth Activities for Children, A Child of God, Earth Tales from Around the World,* and *The Crimson Elf.* His awards include the Aesop Prize, NAPPA Gold and Silver Awards and a Storytelling World Award. Michael travels widely from his home in Vermont, performing and presenting programs and workshops. His website is www.p-e-a-c-e.net.

## *Spirituality of the Seasons*

**Autumn:** A Spiritual Biography of the Season
*Edited by Gary Schmidt and Susan M. Felch; Illustrations by Mary Azarian*
Rejoice in autumn as a time of preparation and reflection. Includes Wendell Berry, David James Duncan, Robert Frost, A. Bartlett Giamatti, E. B. White, P. D. James, Julian of Norwich, Garret Keizer, Tracy Kidder, Anne Lamott, May Sarton.
6 x 9, 320 pp, 5 b/w illus., Quality PB, 978-1-59473-118-1 **$18.99**
HC, 978-1-59473-005-4 **$22.99**

**Spring:** A Spiritual Biography of the Season
*Edited by Gary Schmidt and Susan M. Felch; Illustrations by Mary Azarian*
Explore the gentle unfurling of spring and reflect on how nature celebrates rebirth and renewal. Includes Jane Kenyon, Lucy Larcom, Harry Thurston, Nathaniel Hawthorne, Noel Perrin, Annie Dillard, Martha Ballard, Barbara Kingsolver, Dorothy Wordsworth, Donald Hall, David Brill, Lionel Basney, Isak Dinesen, Paul Laurence Dunbar.
6 x 9, 352 pp, 6 b/w illus., HC, 978-1-59473-114-3 **$21.99**

**Summer:** A Spiritual Biography of the Season
*Edited by Gary Schmidt and Susan M. Felch; Illustrations by Barry Moser*
"A sumptuous banquet.... These selections lift up an exquisite wholeness found within an everyday sophistication."— ★ *Publishers Weekly* starred review
Includes Anne Lamott, Luci Shaw, Ray Bradbury, Richard Selzer, Thomas Lynch, Walt Whitman, Carl Sandburg, Sherman Alexie, Madeleine L'Engle, Jamaica Kincaid.
6 x 9, 304 pp, 5 b/w illus., HC, 978-1-59473-083-2 **$21.99**

**Winter:** A Spiritual Biography of the Season
*Edited by Gary Schmidt and Susan M. Felch; Illustrations by Barry Moser*
"This outstanding anthology features top-flight nature and spirituality writers on the fierce, inexorable season of winter.... Remarkably lively and warm, despite the icy subject." — ★ *Publishers Weekly* starred review.
Includes Will Campbell, Rachel Carson, Annie Dillard, Donald Hall, Ron Hansen, Jane Kenyon, Jamaica Kincaid, Barry Lopez, Kathleen Norris, John Updike, E. B. White.
6 x 9, 288 pp, 6 b/w illus., Deluxe PB w/flaps, 978-1-893361-92-8 **$18.95**
HC, 978-1-893361-53-9 **$21.95**

## *Spirituality / Animal Companions*

### Blessing the Animals
Prayers and Ceremonies to Celebrate God's Creatures, Wild and Tame
*Edited by Lynn L. Caruso*
A compilation of prayers, poetry and blessings for and about animals. Includes St. Francis of Assisi, Galway Kinnell, Evelyn Underhill, Rabindranath Tagore, Elizabeth Barrett Browning, Walt Whitman, Joy Harjo, Rumi.
5 x 7¼, 256 pp, HC, 978-1-59473-145-7 **$19.99**

### What Animals Can Teach Us about Spirituality
Inspiring Lessons from Wild and Tame Creatures    *by Diana L. Guerrero*
Ideal for readers who are interested in how animals touch the soul, and for those who have asked, "Do animals have souls?"
6 x 9, 176 pp, Quality PB, 978-1-893361-84-3 **$16.95**

*Or phone, fax, mail or e-mail to:* SKYLIGHT PATHS Publishing
Sunset Farm Offices, Route 4 • P.O. Box 237 • Woodstock, Vermont 05091
Tel: (802) 457-4000 • Fax: (802) 457-4004 • www.skylightpaths.com
*Credit card orders:* (800) 962-4544 (8:30AM–5:30PM ET Monday–Friday)
*Generous discounts on quantity orders. SATISFACTION GUARANTEED. Prices subject to change.*

# Children's Spirituality

ENDORSED BY CATHOLIC, PROTESTANT, JEWISH, AND BUDDHIST RELIGIOUS LEADERS

**Remembering My Grandparent:** A Kid's Own Grief Workbook in the Christian Tradition   *by Nechama Liss-Levinson, PhD, and Rev. Molly Phinney Baskette, MDiv*
8 x 10, 48 pp, 2-color text, HC, 978-1-59473-212-6  **$16.99**  *For ages 7–13*

**Does God Ever Sleep?**   *by Joan Sauro, CSJ; Full-color photos*
A charming nighttime reminder that God is always present in our lives.
10 x 8½, 32 pp, Quality PB, Full-color photos, 978-1-59473-110-5  **$8.99**  *For ages 3–6*

**Does God Forgive Me?**   *by August Gold; Full-color photos by Diane Hardy Waller*
Gently shows how God forgives all that we do if we are truly sorry.
10 x 8½, 32 pp, Quality PB, Full-color photos, 978-1-59473-142-6  **$8.99**  *For ages 3–6*

**God Said Amen**   *by Sandy Eisenberg Sasso; Full-color illus. by Avi Katz*
A warm and inspiring tale of two kingdoms that shows us that we need only reach out to each other to find the answers to our prayers.
9 x 12, 32 pp, HC, Full-color illus., 978-1-58023-080-3  **$16.95**
*For ages 4 & up (a Jewish Lights book)*

**How Does God Listen?**   *by Kay Lindahl; Full-color photos by Cynthia Maloney*
How do we know when God is listening to us? Children will find the answers to these questions as they engage their senses while the story unfolds, learning how God listens in the wind, waves, clouds, hot chocolate, perfume, our tears and our laughter.
10 x 8½, 32 pp, Quality PB, Full-color photos, 978-1-59473-084-9  **$8.99**  *For ages 3–6*

**In God's Hands**   *by Lawrence Kushner and Gary Schmidt; Full-color illus. by Matthew J. Baeck*
9 x 12, 32 pp, Full-color illus., HC, 978-1-58023-224-1  **$16.99**  *For ages 5 & up  (a Jewish Lights book)*

**In God's Name**   *by Sandy Eisenberg Sasso; Full-color illus. by Phoebe Stone*
Like an ancient myth in its poetic text and vibrant illustrations, this award-winning modern fable about the search for God's name celebrates the diversity and, at the same time, the unity of all the people of the world.
9 x 12, 32 pp, HC, Full-color illus., 978-1-879045-26-2  **$16.99**
*For ages 4 & up (a Jewish Lights book)*

Also available in Spanish: **El nombre de Dios**
9 x 12, 32 pp, HC, Full-color illus., 978-1-893361-63-8  **$16.95**

**In Our Image:** God's First Creatures
*by Nancy Sohn Swartz; Full-color illus. by Melanie Hall*
A playful new twist on the Genesis story—from the perspective of the animals. Celebrates the interconnectedness of nature and the harmony of all living things.   9 x 12, 32 pp, HC, Full-color illus., 978-1-879045-99-6  **$16.95**
*For ages 4 & up (a Jewish Lights book)*

**Noah's Wife:** The Story of Naamah
*by Sandy Eisenberg Sasso; Full-color illus. by Bethanne Andersen*
This new story, based on an ancient text, opens readers' religious imaginations to new ideas about the well-known story of the Flood. When God tells Noah to bring the animals of the world onto the ark, God also calls on Naamah, Noah's wife, to save each plant on Earth.
9 x 12, 32 pp, HC, Full-color illus., 978-1-58023-134-3  **$16.95**
*For ages 4 & up (a Jewish Lights book)*

Also available: **Naamah:** Noah's Wife (A Board Book)
*by Sandy Eisenberg Sasso; Full-color illus. by Bethanne Andersen*
5 x 5, 24 pp, Board Book, Full-color illus., 978-1-893361-56-0  **$7.99**  *For ages 0–4*

**Where Does God Live?**   *by August Gold and Matthew J. Perlman*
Using simple, everyday examples that children can relate to, this colorful book helps young readers develop a personal understanding of God.
10 x 8½, 32 pp, Quality PB, Full-color photo illus., 978-1-893361-39-3  **$8.99**  *For ages 3–6*

# Spirituality

**Jewish Spirituality:** A Brief Introduction for Christians   *by Lawrence Kushner*
5½ x 8½, 112 pp, Quality PB, 978-1-58023-150-3 **$12.95**  *(a Jewish Lights book)*

**Journeys of Simplicity:** Traveling Light with Thomas Merton, Bashō, Edward Abbey, Annie Dillard & Others  *by Philip Harnden*  5 x 7¼, 128 pp, HC, 978-1-893361-76-8 **$16.95**

**Keeping Spiritual Balance As We Grow Older:** More than 65 Creative Ways to Use Purpose, Prayer, and the Power of Spirit to Build a Meaningful Retirement
*by Molly and Bernie Srode*  8 x 8, 224 pp, Quality PB, 978-1-59473-042-9 **$16.99**

**The Monks of Mount Athos:** A Western Monk's Extraordinary Spiritual Journey on Eastern Holy Ground  *by M. Basil Pennington, ocso; Foreword by Archimandrite Dionysios*
6 x 9, 256 pp, 10+ b/w line drawings, Quality PB, 978-1-893361-78-2 **$18.95**

**One God Clapping:** The Spiritual Path of a Zen Rabbi  *by Alan Lew with Sherrill Jaffe*
5½ x 8½, 336 pp, Quality PB, 978-1-58023-115-2 **$16.95**  *(a Jewish Lights book)*

**Prayer for People Who Think Too Much:** A Guide to Everyday, Anywhere Prayer from the World's Faith Traditions  *by Mitch Finley*
5½ x 8½, 224 pp, Quality PB, 978-1-893361-21-8 **$16.99**; HC, 978-1-893361-00-3 **$21.95**

**Show Me Your Way:** The Complete Guide to Exploring Interfaith Spiritual Direction
*by Howard A. Addison*  5½ x 8½, 240 pp, Quality PB, 978-1-893361-41-6 **$16.95**

**Spirituality 101:** The Indispensable Guide to Keeping—or Finding—Your Spiritual Life on Campus  *by Harriet L. Schwartz, with contributions from college students at nearly thirty campuses across the United States*  6 x 9, 272 pp, Quality PB, 978-1-59473-000-9 **$16.99**

**Spiritually Incorrect:** Finding God in All the Wrong Places  *by Dan Wakefield; Illus. by Marian DelVecchio*  5½ x 8½, 192 pp, b/w illus., Quality PB, 978-1-59473-137-2 **$15.99**

**Spiritual Manifestos:** Visions for Renewed Religious Life in America from Young Spiritual Leaders of Many Faiths  *Edited by Niles Elliot Goldstein; Preface by Martin E. Marty*
6 x 9, 256 pp, HC, 978-1-893361-09-6 **$21.95**

**A Walk with Four Spiritual Guides:** Krishna, Buddha, Jesus, and Ramakrishna
*by Andrew Harvey*  5½ x 8½, 192 pp, 10 b/w photos & illus., Quality PB, 978-1-59473-138-9 **$15.99**

**What Matters:** Spiritual Nourishment for Head and Heart
*by Frederick Franck*  5 x 7¼, 128 pp, 50+ b/w illus., HC, 978-1-59473-013-9 **$16.99**

**Who Is My God?, 2nd Edition:** An Innovative Guide to Finding Your Spiritual Identity
*Created by the Editors at SkyLight Paths*  6 x 9, 160 pp, Quality PB, 978-1-59473-014-6 **$15.99**

# Spirituality—A Week Inside

**Come and Sit:** A Week Inside Meditation Centers
*by Marcia Z. Nelson; Foreword by Wayne Teasdale*
The insider's guide to meditation in a variety of different spiritual traditions—Buddhist, Hindu, Christian, Jewish, and Sufi traditions.
6 x 9, 224 pp, b/w photos, Quality PB, 978-1-893361-35-5 **$16.95**

**Lighting the Lamp of Wisdom:** A Week Inside a Yoga Ashram
*by John Ittner; Foreword by Dr. David Frawley*
This insider's guide to Hindu spiritual life takes you into a typical week of retreat inside a yoga ashram to demystify the experience and show you what to expect.
6 x 9, 192 pp, 10+ b/w photos, Quality PB, 978-1-893361-52-2 **$15.95**

**Making a Heart for God:** A Week Inside a Catholic Monastery
*by Dianne Aprile; Foreword by Brother Patrick Hart, ocso*
Takes you to the Abbey of Gethsemani—the Trappist monastery in Kentucky that was home to author Thomas Merton—to explore the details.
6 x 9, 224 pp, b/w photos, Quality PB, 978-1-893361-49-2 **$16.95**

**Waking Up:** A Week Inside a Zen Monastery
*by Jack Maguire; Foreword by John Daido Loori, Roshi*
An essential guide to what it's like to spend a week inside a Zen Buddhist monastery.
6 x 9, 224 pp, b/w photos, Quality PB, 978-1-893361-55-3 **$16.95**
HC, 978-1-893361-13-3 **$21.95**

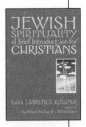
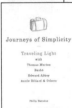
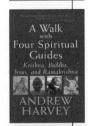

# Spirituality & Crafts

**The Knitting Way:** A Guide to Spiritual Self-Discovery
*by Linda Skolnik and Janice MacDaniels*
7 x 9, 240 pp, Quality PB, 978-1-59473-079-5 **$16.99**

**The Quilting Path**
A Guide to Spiritual Discovery through Fabric, Thread and Kabbalah
*by Louise Silk*
7 x 9, 192 pp, Quality PB, 978-1-59473-206-5 **$16.99**

# Spiritual Practice

**Divining the Body**
Reclaim the Holiness of Your Physical Self  *by Jan Phillips*
A practical and inspiring guidebook for connecting the body and soul in spiritual practice. Leads you into a milieu of reverence, mystery and delight, helping you discover your body as a pathway to the Divine.
8 x 8, 256 pp, Quality PB, 978-1-59473-080-1 **$16.99**

**Finding Time for the Timeless:** Spirituality in the Workweek
*by John McQuiston II*
Simple, refreshing stories that provide you with examples of how you can refocus and enrich your daily life using prayer or meditation, ritual and other forms of spiritual practice.  5½ x 6¾, 208 pp, HC, 978-1-59473-035-1 **$17.99**

**The Gospel of Thomas**
A Guidebook for Spiritual Practice  *by Ron Miller; Translations by Stevan Davies*
An innovative guide to bring a new spiritual classic into daily life.
6 x 9, 160 pp, Quality PB, 978-1-59473-047-4 **$14.99**

**Earth, Water, Fire, and Air:** Essential Ways of Connecting to Spirit
*by Cait Johnson*  6 x 9, 224 pp, HC, 978-1-893361-65-2 **$19.95**

**Everyday Herbs in Spiritual Life:** A Guide to Many Practices
*by Ana Hernández and Susan F. Jones*  5½ x 8½, 176 pp, Quality PB, 978-1-59473-174-7 **$16.99**

**Labyrinths from the Outside In:** Walking to Spiritual Insight—A Beginner's Guide
*by Donna Schaper and Carole Ann Camp*
6 x 9, 208 pp, b/w illus. and photos, Quality PB, 978-1-893361-18-8 **$16.95**

**Practicing the Sacred Art of Listening:** A Guide to Enrich Your Relationships
and Kindle Your Spiritual Life—The Listening Center Workshop
*by Kay Lindahl*  8 x 8, 176 pp, Quality PB, 978-1-893361-85-0 **$16.95**

**Releasing the Creative Spirit:** Unleash the Creativity in Your Life
*by Dan Wakefield*  7 x 10, 256 pp, Quality PB, 978-1-893361-36-2 **$16.95**

**The Sacred Art of Bowing:** Preparing to Practice
*by Andi Young*  5½ x 8½, 128 pp, b/w illus., Quality PB, 978-1-893361-82-9 **$14.95**

**The Sacred Art of Chant:** Preparing to Practice
*by Ana Hernández*  5½ x 8½, 192 pp, Quality PB, 978-1-59473-036-8 **$15.99**

**The Sacred Art of Fasting:** Preparing to Practice
*by Thomas Ryan, CSP*  5½ x 8½, 192 pp, Quality PB, 978-1-59473-078-8 **$15.99**

**The Sacred Art of Forgiveness:** Forgiving Ourselves and Others through God's Grace
*by Marcia Ford*  8 x 8, 176 pp, Quality PB, 978-1-59473-175-4 **$16.99**

**The Sacred Art of Listening:** Forty Reflections for Cultivating a Spiritual Practice
*by Kay Lindahl; Illustrations by Amy Schnapper*
8 x 8, 160 pp, b/w illus., Quality PB, 978-1-893361-44-7 **$16.99**

**The Sacred Art of Lovingkindness:** Preparing to Practice
*by Rabbi Rami Shapiro; Foreword by Marcia Ford*
5½ x 8½, 176 pp, Quality PB, 978-1-59473-151-8 **$16.99**

**Sacred Speech:** A Practical Guide for Keeping Spirit in Your Speech
*by Rev. Donna Schaper*  6 x 9, 176 pp, Quality PB, 978-1-59473-068-9 **$15.99**
HC, 978-1-893361-74-4 **$21.95**

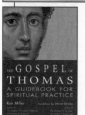
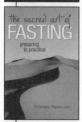

# Midrash Fiction / Folktales

### Abraham's Bind & Other Bible Tales of Trickery, Folly, Mercy and Love  by Michael J. Caduto
New retellings of episodes in the lives of familiar biblical characters explore relevant life lessons.
6 x 9, 224 pp, HC, 978-1-59473-186-0 **$19.99**

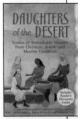

### Daughters of the Desert: Stories of Remarkable Women from Christian, Jewish and Muslim Traditions  by Claire Rudolf Murphy, Meghan Nuttall Sayres, Mary Cronk Farrell, Sarah Conover and Betsy Wharton
Breathes new life into the old tales of our female ancestors in faith. Uses traditional scriptural passages as starting points, then with vivid detail fills in historical context and place. Chapters reveal the voices of Sarah, Hagar, Huldah, Esther, Salome, Mary Magdalene, Lydia, Khadija, Fatima and many more. Historical fiction ideal for readers of all ages. Quality paperback includes reader's discussion guide.
5½ x 8½, 192 pp, Quality PB, 978-1-59473-106-8 **$14.99**
HC, 192 pp, 978-1-893361-72-0 **$19.95**

### The Triumph of Eve & Other Subversive Bible Tales
*by Matt Biers-Ariel*
Many people were taught and remember only a one-dimensional Bible. These engaging retellings are the antidote to this—they're witty, often hilarious, always profound, and invite you to grapple with questions and issues that are often hidden in the original text.
5½ x 8½, 192 pp, HC, 978-1-59473-040-5 **$19.99**

### Also avail.: The Triumph of Eve Teacher's Guide
8½ x 11, 44 pp, PB, 978-1-59473-152-5 **$8.99**

### Wisdom in the Telling
Finding Inspiration and Grace in Traditional Folktales and Myths Retold
*by Lorraine Hartin-Gelardi*
6 x 9, 224 pp, HC, 978-1-59473-185-3 **$19.99**

# Religious Etiquette / Reference

### How to Be a Perfect Stranger, 4th Edition: The Essential Religious Etiquette Handbook  Edited by Stuart M. Matlins and Arthur J. Magida
The indispensable guidebook to help the well-meaning guest when visiting other people's religious ceremonies. A straightforward guide to the rituals and celebrations of the major religions and denominations in the United States and Canada from the perspective of an interested guest of any other faith, based on information obtained from authorities of each religion. Belongs in every living room, library and office. Covers:

**African American Methodist Churches • Assemblies of God • Bahá'í • Baptist • Buddhist • Christian Church (Disciples of Christ) • Christian Science (Church of Christ, Scientist) • Churches of Christ • Episcopalian and Anglican • Hindu • Islam • Jehovah's Witnesses • Jewish • Lutheran • Mennonite/Amish • Methodist • Mormon (Church of Jesus Christ of Latter-day Saints) • Native American/First Nations • Orthodox Churches • Pentecostal Church of God • Presbyterian • Quaker (Religious Society of Friends) • Reformed Church in America/Canada • Roman Catholic • Seventh-day Adventist • Sikh • Unitarian Universalist • United Church of Canada • United Church of Christ**
6 x 9, 432 pp, Quality PB, 978-1-59473-140-2 **$19.99**

### The Perfect Stranger's Guide to Funerals and Grieving Practices: A Guide to Etiquette in Other People's Religious Ceremonies  Edited by Stuart M. Matlins
6 x 9, 240 pp, Quality PB, 978-1-893361-20-1 **$16.95**

### The Perfect Stranger's Guide to Wedding Ceremonies: A Guide to Etiquette in Other People's Religious Ceremonies  Edited by Stuart M. Matlins
6 x 9, 208 pp, Quality PB, 978-1-893361-19-5 **$16.95**

## About SKYLIGHT PATHS Publishing

SkyLight Paths Publishing is creating a place where people of different spiritual traditions come together for challenge and inspiration, a place where we can help each other understand the mystery that lies at the heart of our existence.

Through spirituality, our religious beliefs are increasingly becoming a part of our lives—rather than *apart* from our lives. While many of us may be more interested than ever in spiritual growth, we may be less firmly planted in traditional religion. Yet, we do want to deepen our relationship to the sacred, to learn from our own as well as from other faith traditions, and to practice in new ways.

SkyLight Paths sees both believers and seekers as a community that increasingly transcends traditional boundaries of religion and denomination—people wanting to learn from each other, *walking together, finding the way.*

For your information and convenience, at the back of this book we have provided a list of other SkyLight Paths books you might find interesting and useful. They cover the following subjects:

| | | |
|---|---|---|
| Buddhism / Zen | Gnosticism | Mysticism |
| Catholicism | Hinduism / | Poetry |
| Children's Books | Vedanta | Prayer |
| Christianity | Inspiration | Religious Etiquette |
| Comparative | Islam / Sufism | Retirement |
| Religion | Judaism / Kabbalah / | Spiritual Biography |
| Current Events | Enneagram | Spiritual Direction |
| Earth-Based | Meditation | Spirituality |
| Spirituality | Midrash Fiction | Women's Interest |
| Global Spiritual | Monasticism | Worship |
| Perspectives | | |

*Or phone, fax, mail or e-mail to:* SKYLIGHT PATHS Publishing
Sunset Farm Offices, Route 4 • P.O. Box 237 • Woodstock, Vermont 05091
Tel: (802) 457-4000 • Fax: (802) 457-4004 • www.skylightpaths.com
*Credit card orders:* (800) 962-4544 (8:30AM–5:30PM ET Monday–Friday)
Generous discounts on quantity orders. SATISFACTION GUARANTEED. Prices subject to change.

# For more information about each book,
# visit our website at www.skylightpaths.com